What people are saying...

"The author writes in a way that takes you on an emotional roller coaster with her. I cried with her during the hard moments and rejoiced at her triumphs. As a young widow myself, reading her description of widowhood felt like she was reading my mind, and putting words to a feeling that I had never been able to. Her story is inspiring to anyone, and resonates even stronger with those who can relate."

—Heather Cruz

"Without warning she became a widow with two small children and her life changed forever. She found herself struggling day to day to control her grief and depression. Determined to not let her circumstances define her, taking one day at a time, one step at a time she fought to overcome her heartache to create a "new normal" for herself, Abby and Ryan. Jen's story is authentic as she candidly shares the struggles that challenged her. She persevered making a place in her heart for peace and happiness once again."

—Stephanie S. Feyler

"Jennifer writes her compelling true story of a young love lost too soon and how she rose from the ashes. This is one of those books, you can't put down and you can't help but to put yourself in her shoes. She faced a situation most of us can't imagine and her ability to write about it in such detail gives readers insight to an unthinkable tragedy. Her story of resiliency is inspiring and this book shows the strength of the human spirit."

—Susie Masten

One Step at a Time moved me to tears more than once. It was written with beautiful transparency and can give hope to anyone feeling broken and at rock bottom. Absolutely encouraging."

—Estee Gleasner

"*One Step at a Time* by Jennifer Steele is a refreshing glimpse into real life. The battle of heartache, depression, life and finally love spring to life in this quick read. Be prepared to laugh, cry and feel incredibly inspired with this story of a young widow trying to seek past the darkness and climb into the light. I would and have recommended this book to everyone that just needs some inspiration in a world where we don't have much. Namaste Jen, you are a diamond!"

—Amy West

"As a person who has experienced tremendous loss, *One Step at a Time* was refreshing, validating, and thought provoking. Many times, I have had the thought of...if only I could explain how I was feeling...this book did exactly that! Jennifer Steele is a gifted writer who is honest and real in this essential book. I would highly recommend this well-written, hope-filled book to everyone. *One Step at a Time* is a must read for supporters, and those who are grieving alike, as it will undoubtedly help you better understand life-changing loss."

—Angel Street

"In *One Step at a Time*, Jennifer Steele takes us on a journey during a period of time that was dark and most certainly felt like a lonely lifetime to the light at the end of the tunnel that makes the reader feel the pressure lifting and hope settling in. Tragedy strikes us all, some far more paramount than others, but the message can be received by everyone-Don't Give Up, you only have to take One Step at a Time!"

—Christine Michael

ONE STEP
AT A TIME

Jennifer C. Steele

ISBN: 9781070952888

Edited by: Lisa Condora, Condora Content

www.happyselfpublisher.com

I dedicate this book to Abigail and Ryan,

I kept going for you.

Love you forever.

TABLE OF CONTENTS

FOREWORD

When people ask me about Jen, my answer is not simple or clear cut, such is life. The simplest answer I could provide you with is that Jen is quiet and reserved. However, if you're asking me for an honest answer (and you are), then you will not get the simplest answer.

Jen is quiet with an awesomely boisterous laugh, but also reserved, yet forward. She is incredibly brave, strong, intelligent, beautiful, funny, a lover of great music, and known to have the freshest dance moves. Jen is also a healer who is generous, spiritual, peaceful, kind, and happy. She is not limited to these, but when I think of her in this present moment, these are the first qualities that come to mind.

Technically speaking, I first met Jen in the fall of 2013 while I was waiting in the lobby before a Combat Fitness class. I remember her seeming unhappy at that moment. About what? I was not sure and it did not feel personal or against anyone around us. I chalked it up to nerves before class. As another friend introduced us, smiles and nods were what both of us supplied the other. In the following months and years leading up to our yoga teacher training, when I saw her in class, we did not speak very much. It was never because we did not click or did not like each other. It was simply due to both our natures and how we were showing up in the world at that time. We were both quiet and reserved.

Fast forward to 2016 and I learned that we both signed up to complete the same two-hundred-hour yoga teacher training. Both of us will still tell anyone to this day that we had NO clue what we were about to embark upon. Little did we know that despite our quiet and reserved natures, we would be thrown (figuratively and literally) into these "self-work" activities during our yoga teacher training. We would have to dig deep, pull up all the cruddy things, and face them. There was zero room for quiet and reserved. No matter how scary it was or how many boxes of tissues we all went through, Jen showed up every time with a bit more bravery than the last. On breaks, I got to see a silly side of Jen. As we shared laughs and snacks, I remember thinking, "Thank goodness she loves laughs and snacks, too." Let's face it. Bravery is damn important in your own self-work, but laughter and snacks are a necessity in that process!

Through the eleven months that it took us to complete the two-hundred hours of teacher training, it was beautiful to watch her showing up and working through the activities. She allowed me (and the others) into her past that led her to the steps she was then taking towards healing. It was clear that the universe decided we should experience pieces of our self-work together in those months.

Ultimately, our journeys and the self-work on those journeys have led us to not only become co-workers as yoga instructors and comrades in life coaching, but also friends.

Jen is a friend, who at times can be quiet and reserved. This time, she has stepped up once more to be her best, brave self to share with you her journey of healing, finding peace, and reconnecting to happiness. One step at a time.

— Amy Roscoe

INTRODUCTION

"During those times when our lives are changing, we may feel out of tune, out of rhythm, out of balance. Out of step. The old picture is being erased so a new one can be drawn. This means things are moving and movement is good. For now, it may feel like you can't find your place, but that's because your place is changing."
Journey to the Heart by Melody Beattie.

July 11, 2012

The day I heard the words, "I'm sorry, we did all that we could, but your husband didn't make it."

The day my life was split into two distinct parts—before and after.

"Young widow" was never on my list of "things I want to be when I grow up." Grieving the loss of my husband was not something I was prepared for. "Till death do us part" was not supposed to happen in my thirties. It was not in the plans to raise our two children on my own. *We* were supposed to do this together and grow old together. This was not the way my life was supposed to go.

Losing my husband unexpectedly at a young age has been one of the most life-altering moments I've ever experienced. The traumatic events of that day have changed me in unimaginable and sometimes indescribable ways. I went to sleep one night, and then the next morning, the entire world as I knew it came crashing down around me. I still may resemble the same person on the outside, but the person I was before that day is gone, laid to rest with my late husband.

No part of this journey has been easy. The majority of the first year after Kevin's loss was spent strictly in survival mode. Everything was a blur and I lived moment-to-moment with no real plan. As the days slowly went by, I was literally just going through the motions. I was stuck in the feeling of fight or flight, while battling severe depression, guilt, and anxiety. There were times I did anything I could to numb the way I was feeling. I questioned every move I made. I tried my best, but I was frantic and my thoughts were fragmented. I went from moments of clarity into what felt like complete insanity in the span of just one afternoon. In the darkest moments, I truly wished it had been me who had died instead of him.

If you made the choice to read this, thank you. Please don't expect a how-to manual on grief or the highlight reel of the journey. This is *my* story, told by me, the way I remember it. My hope is that by sharing my ups and downs and all the realness, I can offer reassurance to others who may share similar experiences or feelings. Looking back, I wish I had someone my age who had been through this type of loss to look to for inspiration. I hope that by making the choice to keep going, I inspire someone else to do the same.

In the spirit of complete transparency, I almost didn't publish this story. I struggled so much with the process of writing this book. I feel in my heart that my story can, and will, help others. Still, it has been quite the emotional roller-coaster. I've had to dig really deep. This introduction alone took me over a month to write. My recycling bin has been full of crumpled papers for months now, and the delete button on my computer should be getting paid overtime.

It has been emotionally trying to come face-to-face with my grief. Reliving some of these painful memories I thought were forever in the past have triggered some rather nasty bouts of depression. Anger that I thought had been laid to rest came bubbling to the surface again at the same intensity as before. If you already have a history of depression, anxiety, or low self-esteem, grief exacerbates all those emotions. There were times I felt it would have been easier for me just to quit. However, if I have learned anything from this whole experience, it's that you must keep going, even when you think you don't have it in you, even if it's just one step. You're stronger than you think you are.

1

THE NIGHTMARE

"The moon split in half and the stars crumbled, falling like
fireworks into the sea. I watched the world fall apart
the day my love left me."
– Christy Ann Martine

"This cannot be real." On my way to the emergency room, those words ran over and over again in my mind.

"Any moment now, this is all going to be over and I am going to wake up from this nightmare."

"This *cannot* be real."

Deep down, I already knew what they were going to say. I was there in our bedroom, right beside him. I heard the sound. Did you know there was a sound? It's called "the death rattle." It's a gurgling noise a person makes in their throat when they are near death, the sound of life leaving the body. It's a sound you don't ever forget. I heard it years before when my father died from brain cancer.

I felt it happen. I felt him leave this earth. I noticed the ambulance sat in front of our house a little too long for it to still be considered an emergency. In my mind, I already knew the truth. Yet, I held onto the smallest shred of hope on the way to the hospital. My heart couldn't accept the reality. This couldn't be happening. Not again. I can't lose him, too.

When I stepped through the emergency room doors, not one person there met my eyes. I thought maybe I was reading too much into things. Maybe I was wrong about everything. Maybe I didn't see or hear what I thought I did. It was rather early in the morning. I am not a doctor. Everything was going to be just fine. It just needed to be. I hoped I would wake up any minute and roll over in bed. He would still be there sound asleep. We would both awaken and then go on with our normal daily routine.

God, how I wanted normal so badly in that moment!

I would get up and drink my coffee. Kevin would be getting dressed for work. I would wish him a good day and kiss him goodbye. Just like any other ordinary day. That would be normal, not this nightmare.

If no one said the words to me, then it's not actually happening, right?

I was in denial.

Unfortunately for me, this was not a scene from a horror movie or some crazy, messed-up, bad dream. I was fully awake. This was indeed happening, whether I wanted to admit it or not. I had a sinking feeling that normal was forever gone from my life, never to be seen or heard from again.

The nurses escorted me to a small, private waiting area toward the back of the emergency room. Kevin's father dropped me off and was waiting in the main lobby for the rest of the family to arrive. I was by myself. The shades were pulled down and there were no magazines or televisions in sight. I briefly thought it was odd that the room was so bare. It seemed so cold, lifeless, and uninviting. It seems strange now that I would notice such irrelevant things on one of the worst days of my life. I think it was my brain's way of trying to distract me from what I knew was inevitably coming.

I was told someone would come in to speak to me shortly. Funny how time can pass so quickly when you are having fun, yet the same small amount of time can seem like an eternity when you are awaiting bad news.

I felt the events of the morning taking a toll on my body and mind. I sat there, as I nervously picked at my fingernails and my legs shook uncontrollably. My mind kicked into overdrive. My inner voice shouted, "Red flags everywhere! I want my husband! Why don't they bring me to his room? When is the part that they tell me he's okay? When can I see him? What is taking so long? SOMETHING IS TERRIBLY WRONG! I can feel it!"

I kept trying to calm myself down to no avail. "No, no, no. Stop it! Stop thinking the worst. You always think the worst. Everything is fine! Maybe he's in surgery or something. Any minute now, they are going to let me see him. Any minute now, they are going to tell me he is going to be okay. Any minute now, this will all be over, and we can all go back home. Yup, any minute now. I'll just close my eyes really tight and then open them again." I tried, but nope, I was still in that dreadful room.

I drifted in and out between moments of shock and moments of clarity. The numbness subsided a bit, and panic started to completely take over. Sensory overload. My body started to tremble all over again. My breath was too heavy and tears stung my eyes. The sounds were too loud. My limbs weren't moving right. There seemed to be a haze around everything. People who walked by seemed robotic, void of any feelings or emotion. I had never felt alone like this before. Even though the hospital was full of people, I didn't feel a connection to anything.

My thoughts became more and more erratic. "There has been some sort of terrible mistake, you see. I can't lose my husband. I just can't. Not me. He's too young. I'm too young. He was fine yesterday. I just talked to him. We have two young children. I can't do this on my own. I can't lose someone else I love. That's just not fair. My heart can't take it. I won't survive this, not without him. This has all been a terrible mistake. Please show me to his room so we can go home and put this awful morning behind us." Over and over, I pleaded in my mind, "Please God, no, don't take him," hoping someone upstairs would hear me and somehow reverse what had been done.

After what felt like an eternity, two people in scrubs entered the room. It was in that moment that my nightmare became a reality. The look on their faces told me everything

I needed to know. As I collapsed onto the floor and started sobbing, they said the words that made it real.

"We're incredibly sorry. There was nothing else we could do."

2

THE DAY EVERYTHING CHANGED

"A thousand moments that I had just taken for granted.
Mostly because I had assumed
there would be a thousand more."
– Morgan Matson

Looking back, there was nothing extraordinary about this day. Nothing stood out to predict that it was going to be different. There were no warning signals or flashing lights to let me know something bad was coming. There were no neon signs to tell me to be prepared for danger ahead. It was basically just another hot, July day.

The kids and I were on summer vacation from school, and Kevin was back to work after using some vacation time. The four of us spent his week off with a few day trips to the beach. We also worked on some projects around the house and relaxed by the pool. We wrapped up the week with a barbecue held by our friends that he had known since high school. They had a party every year to celebrate Independence Day, and this year was no exception. Hamburgers, hot dogs, and beer can chicken were on the menu. We played horseshoes, washers, and watched the fireworks in the backyard with the kids. It had become a tradition. In our ten and a half years of marriage, we had only missed this annual celebration a few times that I can remember.

I had recently received a promotion to Cafeteria Manager at the elementary school our children attended. One of the many perks of the promotion was an invitation to a school nutrition convention in Colorado, so I was getting prepared for my upcoming business trip. I was excited and a bit anxious to start my new position in the fall and looked forward to the opportunity to connect with some of the other managers before the school year started. More than anything else, I was happy to be able to contribute more financially at home and relieve some of our stress. It would be an adjustment for all of us. Up until then, I only worked part-time and was a full-time stay-at-home mom.

I felt a little nervous about the trip because this was the first time I was traveling out of state, away from the kids. It was also the longest I would be away from Kevin since we got married. We didn't spend much time apart. We were homebodies for the most part. We were content to swim in the pool, barbecue with friends, and spend time with our kids, families, friends, and of course, each other.

Since Kevin was back to work, I made plans to drop our kids off at my mom's house. They were going to stay with her for a few days while I was gone, and then they were headed on a camping trip with Kevin's family. It was supposed to be a fun few weeks for them to get spoiled by their grandparents before they had to start thinking about school supply lists and book-bag shopping.

Summer vacation was in full swing and we were living it up. I drove the hour to spend time with my mom and my sister for the afternoon. Once the kids were settled, we said our goodbyes and I was on my way back home to start packing for my trip. Kevin and I spoke earlier that morning and decided we would have a date night since it would just be the two of us. When he got home from work, we planned to grab some dinner and spend some quality time before I left for a few days.

On the way home, I stopped at the store for a few items. I bought travel toothpaste, a few new shirts, a loaf of bread, peanut butter, jelly, and some small bags of chips for Kevin's lunches. (I used to joke with him that he had the same lunch as all the kindergarten students at my school.) I even splurged and bought one of those pop-up tents because our gazebo had blown over and ripped the previous weekend in one of those freak summer thunderstorms. Just your normal, everyday, run-of-the-mill stuff. I drove home with the windows down, as I sang along to the radio, not having a clue what was in store for my future.

I waved at my neighbor mowing her lawn as I pulled into our neighborhood. I pulled the van into the driveway and brought my new purchases inside. My plan was to hurry and finish some household chores before I got ready for dinner, so I wouldn't have to worry about them when we returned home. I put away toys, switched the laundry, made the beds, cleaned the bugs from the pool, and watered the garden. I always wanted a vegetable garden. Kevin and the kids sweetly surprised me earlier that year for Mother's Day with my own little patch in the backyard.

When I came back inside, I noticed two missed calls and a voicemail on my cell phone. I got a little nervous when I saw they were from Kevin because he wasn't supposed to make calls from work. I tried to call him back immediately, but he didn't answer, so I hung up and listened to his voicemail message. I could tell something was wrong. It was out of character for him to get overly excited. He was normally very steady. He wasn't dramatic and didn't complain much about anything. He was a very even keel, go-with-the-flow kind of guy. However, his message today had a hint of panic behind his words. It was very short and to the point. He was having extremely bad pains in his chest and he was on his way to the hospital.

Crazy how life can change in an instant.

The hospital was only a few miles from where he worked, but about an hour away from our house. I kept trying, but I couldn't reach him by phone, so I spent that drive concocting every worst-case scenario I could possibly think of. The last time I got a phone call like that, it was my mom saying they thought my dad suffered a stroke. Four months after that call, my dad was gone. Terminal brain cancer. That was my only reference to what was occurring now.

I tried to keep it together, not well, but I tried. As I drove by myself to the hospital, unsure of what I was about to walk into, I focused on not going over the speed limit and told myself everything was fine.

When I finally arrived, I made my way to the front desk of the emergency department and gave my name to a staff member. I was buzzed into the triage area and told Kevin was in one of the rooms. I walked around for a bit, looked at the names on each board, and then finally found his name. However, he wasn't in the room at the moment, so I sat in one of the chairs and waited for someone to come tell me where my husband was.

Although it seemed like an eternity, it was probably only about ten minutes before they wheeled Kevin in. I was so relieved to see him. He was very anxious and appeared to still be in a lot of pain. After the doctors left the room, I asked him to fill me in on what was going on. He said he was at work on a call with a customer, when suddenly he felt like he had been shot in the stomach. The doctors ran multiple tests when he got to the hospital, but couldn't find the source of his pain. They monitored him and gave him medicine to keep him comfortable for the time being. After several hours, the doctors came in and gave us discharge instructions. They said they didn't feel it was anything serious or life-threatening and told him to follow up with his primary doctor in the morning.

Briefly, I felt uncomfortable taking him home because we really had no answers as to what was causing the pain, but I thought maybe I was just being nervous as per usual. Kevin said he was tired and that he just wanted to go home. I was assured there was nothing else that could be done that evening, so I tried to put my anxious feelings at ease. We gathered his belongings, left the emergency room, and headed home.

After what was a very long day for both of us, we finally pulled into our driveway shortly before midnight. Kevin went inside while I took care of the dog and cat. We changed into our pajamas, brushed our teeth, and climbed into bed. I remember even being somewhat upset that our date night had gotten ruined. How selfish of me, huh?

Looking back, I wish I would have known it was our last night together. I would have made sure he knew how much I loved him. I would have held him a little tighter and been sure I kissed him good night. Truthfully, I'm not even sure if I did.

I was able to sleep a little, but it was a mostly restless night. Every time Kevin would shift his weight, I would ask if he was okay, to which he would respond, "It still kind of hurts" or "Feels about the same." I felt helpless because I couldn't do anything to take his pain away. Since I was getting on my own nerves, I could only imagine how annoying I was to him.

We planned to call the doctor first thing in the morning to try to get some answers.

We never got the chance to make that call.

At around six a.m., I awoke to an empty bed, feeling groggy from the restless night. I vaguely remember that I heard him in the kitchen open the cabinet and then the sound of water in the sink. I thought to myself, "Oh good, he's up. He must be feeling better."

He came back in the bedroom and climbed into bed. I started to roll over to ask how he was feeling, but I felt him stiffen. It was in that instant that all of the air left his body. The rattle. God, no! I screamed out his name and started to shake him. I tried everything I could to wake him up.

I scrambled out of bed, grabbed the phone off the dresser, and called 911. As I frantically screamed into the phone at the dispatcher, I started chest compressions. "What should I do? He's not waking up. What do I do? What do I do?"

I felt the room spin around me. Still, I tried to keep my composure, for his sake. I had to help him. I had to save him. I yelled to the dispatcher that it wasn't working. I needed help. I couldn't get the right amount of pressure on the mattress, so I had to pull him to the floor. I continued the chest compressions until I heard the doorbell ring.

I ran to the front door. The paramedics asked where he was and then rushed past me down the hall. They were followed closely by two police officers who started questioning me in the front room of our home. They asked me the same things repetitively, trying to obtain all the details of what happened. "Tell me again, ma'am, how old is your husband? Has anything like this happened before?" I felt like I was watching a scene from a movie.

An ambulance sat on the street, in front of our house, and a stretcher accompanied it on the front lawn. Everything felt so wrong and out of place. My body was present in the room, but it felt as if I was watching it all happen to someone else. The questions kept coming, but all I could focus on were the beeps and voice from the defibrillator in the bedroom and the paramedics saying, "Clear."

He never regained consciousness that I am aware of. They brought in the stretcher and transported him outside to the ambulance. I started to follow them out, and one of the officers stopped me on the front steps. She told me I wasn't permitted to ride in the ambulance with him and I would have to follow them or have someone else take me to the hospital. "Wait a minute, what? That's my husband in there. What do you mean I can't go with him?" They shut the door and walked back to their cars as I stood there, hopelessly staring out the window.

I felt like I was frozen in time. I stood in my living room, trying to make some sense out of what just happened. "What do I do now?"

I called my father-in-law because I knew he was home and lived the closest to us. I told him Kevin had been taken by ambulance to the hospital and I needed a ride, as I wasn't able to drive in my current state. I didn't go into details as to what happened because I couldn't bring myself to say the words out loud. Nothing had been confirmed, so I was still able to hope, right?

After I hung up the phone, I sat there for a moment and debated calling my mom. I slowly dialed the number, and when I heard her voice, I was able to briefly snap out of the fog. That was the first time I said the words, "Mom, I think...he's gone. Kevin's gone." She screamed into the phone, "No! No! No! What do you mean?" She didn't want to believe it, either. She gave the phone to my sister, and at that moment, the severity of what happened suddenly hit me. I can't remember what I said to either of them after that point. This was the beginning of my old self starting to slowly slip away.

I could feel everything start to crumble down around me, and there was nothing I could do to stop it. My knees buckled and my head felt scrambled. I knew I needed to get dressed, put my contacts in, and brush my teeth, but I couldn't remember where anything was. I kept walking around in circles, unsure of what to do with myself. I felt like a visitor in a foreign country, a stranger in my own house. I ran into the bathroom and vomited over and over again, sounds coming out of me that I am not sure were human. After that episode, I was briefly able to pull myself together just long enough to get dressed. Little did I know then that this was just the beginning of the trauma roller-coaster ride of emotions.

I waited by the front door for Kevin's dad to arrive, still holding onto that little shred of hope that on the way to the hospital, the paramedics were able to bring him back. I was clinging onto hope with everything I had.

I envisioned a miracle occurring. It happens every

day, right? They bring people back all the time. Kevin is a good husband and father, a good friend to all, a good employee, son, and brother. It couldn't be his time yet. God wouldn't take him from us. Right?

No matter how hard I tried to deny it with my mind, I already knew in my heart he was gone. I couldn't feel his presence with me anymore.

3

SAYING GOODBYE

"Words seem so feeble in moments like these. Life is so precious and death such a thief. The depths of your pain I cannot comprehend, but I'll stand alongside you in the darkness, my friend. Love is a bond that death cannot part. Gone from your arms, but still held in your heart."
– John Mark Green

After they delivered the news to me that my thirty-six-year-old husband was no longer alive, they asked if I wanted to go into the room and say goodbye.

Nope! I would not like to do that. Is there an alternative? A different choice, perhaps? One in which I get to go back to the same life I had yesterday, where I was shopping at Walmart and packing for my trip?

If I had a choice of what I would like to actually do, I would snuggle up in my alive husband's arms and tell him about the terrible morning I just had. I would like for him to comfort me and tell me that everything was going to be all right. I would like to be anywhere but here in this moment. I would like to choose that option instead. Option B, please.

I walked into the room by myself, as no one else had been given the terrible news of his passing yet. His body was lying on the stretcher with a breathing tube still in his throat and he was covered to his chest with a white sheet. Even though I could see him there, I still felt at any moment someone was going to tell me he was someone else's husband who had passed away that morning. A terrible mistake had been made and Kevin is actually in the next room, alive and well and ready to go home. It still wasn't computing in my brain that he was gone. They told us last night that his symptoms were not serious. He was supposed to go to the doctor this morning.

Now he was gone? It just couldn't be.

I didn't want to say goodbye. Those words made it final. They meant that I had accepted it in some way. Once I said goodbye, I couldn't take it back. I wanted to stay in the land of denial. I sat in the doorway and debated going back to the waiting room. I wanted a do-over and to skip the "he didn't make it" part.

Hospital staff wandered in and out of the room, but I didn't budge. They asked me questions, but I can't remember what they said or asked. I still felt like I was watching it all happen to someone else. It was such a strange sensation to feel so disconnected from my own body. I think it was the only reason I survived that day. For if I had allowed myself to feel it all at once, surely my heart would have broken into a million pieces and I would have been on a stretcher in the next room myself.

It felt like five forevers before I finally got the courage to walk over and sit next to him. It didn't feel like him anymore. His spirit was already gone. All that was left on that table was a lifeless body. Kevin, as I knew him, had left me at the house.

I was afraid to touch him. I didn't know what to say. I just sat there, stared at him, and wondered why this all had happened. Nothing felt like "the right thing to do", so I did and said nothing. I was numb. I kept hearing his last breath. What a horrible sound. The scenario played on repeat, over and over again in my mind, banging in my head like a drum.

I remember when his family arrived. Parents should never have to say goodbye to their child. It's not the natural order of things. Siblings should never have to kiss their older brother goodbye forever. It was such a painful thing to witness.

That is when I felt the first pangs of guilt and shame. I questioned if this was my fault somehow. I shouldn't have taken him home last night. I should have listened to my gut. I should have asked more questions. I should have been able to save him. I tried so hard, but I couldn't.

I just sat there beside him because I didn't know what else to do. I still couldn't bring myself to say goodbye. I don't think I ever actually did. The medical examiner came in and said they were required to take his body for an autopsy to determine the cause of death. They wheeled him out and then asked me to leave.

I didn't even know where I was supposed to go. I didn't want to return to the home that had felt so safe just yesterday. Now all I could think of was death and how I never wanted to go back there again. How could I go back to the place that he took his last breath? How will I be able to step foot in our room again or sleep in our bed? I felt another wave of nausea creeping over me. I had no idea what to do or where to turn. I felt exposed to the world. Unsafe, alone, and afraid.

4

THE END OF THE AMERICAN DREAM

*"It's hard to turn the page when you know someone won't
be in the next chapter, but the story must go on."*
— Humble the Poet

After I left the hospital, the fog rolled into my mind, thicker
and thicker. Much later, I learned this is a defense
mechanism that our brain turns on to allow us to continue
to live after experiencing devastating events. All processing
shuts down except for survival protocol; only bits and pieces
of memories are let in at a time. It felt like a dream world.
Everything strange and unfamiliar. Nothing made sense. The
life that I had been so sure of before seemed so different
now. The simplest of tasks felt impossible to manage.

Thousands of questions hammered in my brain. All I
thought was how I couldn't do this again. Not again. I can't

pull myself out of the hole. Kevin helped me so much after the death of my dad. He kept me going when I wanted to stay in bed all day.

How am I supposed to get through this without him? What am I supposed to do next? Why is this happening to me?

And then it hit me like a semi-truck. I have to tell my children—who are ten and seven—that their dad, their hero and provider, who they saw yesterday before they went to their grandmother's house, is now gone. What little was left of my heart shattered right at that moment. As their parent, I was supposed to protect them and keep them safe from hurt and harm. Now I had to deliver news to them that would hurt them more deeply than anything ever had before. This wasn't a scraped knee or a cold. This wasn't, "We can't afford to get you that bike for Christmas this year" or "You didn't make the soccer team." This was life-altering pain. Pain you don't get over. Pain that becomes a part of your existence. Pain that attaches to your soul. Pain that changes who you are.

I lost my dad when I was twenty-five-years-old. He battled cancer, but the cancer won. It was the hardest thing I had ever been through. I got the chance to say goodbye to him. I got the chance to prepare for his death, not that it made it any easier in the end. I *knew* this pain. I carried it with me every day. I wouldn't have given it to my worst enemy. Now I had to watch my children experience that same pain, and to rub extra salt in the wound, I had to be the one to tell them the horrible news. I thought things couldn't possibly get any worse, but I was wrong. That was worse than the loss itself. I would have given anything in that moment to take their pain and carry it all as my own.

I was an adult. It was going to be a long, hard process for me, but I had an understanding of death. I knew you got through it somehow. I previously lost grandparents, aunts, and my dad. My daughter was three and my son was two weeks old when my father passed. This was their first real experience with death—and it was their father, the most important man in their lives. They say grief is the price of love. Love with no place to go. It's a terrible price to pay.

I couldn't put it off any longer. This wasn't going to go away if I avoided it long enough. I had to tell them, so we could start picking through the pieces of the wreckage that was now life. I made the phone call to my mom and asked her to please bring the kids to me at Kevin's parents' home. I needed to be the one to tell them what happened. For the next hour, my stomach was in knots. I alternated between staring blankly at the wall and crying so hard I shook the room.

What do I even say to them? Can we just pretend he is on a trip for a while? I can't hurt them like this. Do they really need to know? I can't do this to them. I can't. God, why? Why would you do this to them?

I heard them come into the house as I sat in the back bedroom, knowing I was about to blindside them with news that would tear their little hearts in pieces. They were excited to see everyone, but a little nervous because they could sense something was off. They weren't supposed to

be home yet. Kids are smart. Even without telling them, they
knew something wasn't quite right.

They came into the bedroom and they were looking
to me for reassurance, both needing something I couldn't
give them at that time. They looked so small standing there
as I looked into their little eyes. They should be playing
outside and learning to ride bikes, not going through this.
This wasn't right. I knelt down and hugged them both tightly,
and with tears in my eyes, I told both of them that their
daddy passed away that morning.

The sounds that came out of them were heart-
wrenching. I will never be able to erase that moment from
my mind. I've experienced a lot of hard things in my life, but
this was hands down the worst of them all. Nothing else
even comes close.

They screamed and cried and denied it as I held their
little bodies close to mine. I knew they would be forever
changed and there was nothing I could do to make it better.
I felt in that moment I had failed them as a mother. I felt so
vulnerable, like I couldn't protect them from anything. There
was nothing I could do to fix this.

I went outside to get some air, and I sat with my two
sisters-in-law in the driveway. I felt completely drained—
physically, emotionally, mentally, and spiritually. I told them
that I had no idea what I was going to do. I didn't know how
I was going to go on. Earlier, when I checked our bank
account balance, we only had a little over two hundred
dollars, and our credit card was almost maxed out. I couldn't
afford a funeral. I couldn't afford to keep the house. We

lived paycheck to paycheck, and we could barely keep it together financially. I didn't sign up to do this on my own. We had a mortgage, car payments, and debt. There was no way I could see to make it work. There was no will. I didn't even know if he had life insurance. No one plans to die in their thirties. We weren't prepared for this. I felt so afraid.

I didn't want to lose everything, but it seemed like that was bound to come next. Everything we built together was bound to be gone. We had the house with the fenced-in backyard and the pool. We had the girl and the boy, and the dog and the cat. We had spent years trying to build the American dream, and I was about to watch it all come tumbling down.

5

CASKETS AND FUNERAL CLOTHES

*"But grief is a walk alone. Others can be there and listen.
But you will walk alone down your own path, at your own
pace, with your sheared-off pain, your raw wounds, your
denial, anger, and bitter loss. You'll come to your own
peace, hopefully...but it will be on your own,
in your own time."*

– Cathy Lamb

As a child, I had lots of hopes and dreams for my life. Some things turned out as planned, but one thing is for certain, I never imagined I would be in my mid-thirties and planning a funeral for my husband. It's not something that you can prepare yourself for. Most people my age were getting married, having babies, buying homes, or celebrating new career choices. Some were getting divorced and some celebrating second weddings. None, not one of them, were planning funerals or learning how to be a young widow.

I have a vague memory of visiting a funeral home. My body was present in the building, but not much else. I'm not sure if I helped make any decisions at all. I have a very similar memory from when we planned my dad's funeral. When the feelings start becoming too much, I check out. I disconnect entirely. It's easier that way.

There wasn't enough air in the building. Do they have special machines that suck the air out of those places? Do they make it extra stuffy and hot on purpose? Is there a class that teaches people how to make the building as uncomfortable as possible? I'm sure it was a lovely place, but to me, it smelled too much like flowers.

The feeling of death in the air was so overwhelming.

I couldn't focus. My breathing was too hard, my heart started to race again, and the room started to feel like it wasn't big enough for all of us. Panic started to become my go-to emotion, and I was not a fan of not having control of my body. I had to leave the room. I think I may have answered some questions about caskets and verses. I even think I helped picked a song, maybe? I don't know. It was too much for my mind to process, and most of that day is gone somewhere in the fog.

Next on the agenda was funeral clothing. What? I have to actually pick out special clothing for this? There was no way I was going shopping to buy funeral clothing for myself and the kids. It just wasn't going to happen. I don't even like clothes shopping on a good day. I didn't even want to shower and put regular clothing on. How would I possibly get through this task?

Luckily for me, my two sisters-in-law jumped in and helped me out with this one. I would have worn a trash bag, for all I cared at that time. I was still in a haze and basically still refusing to believe it was all real. I had not even been home yet, except to grab a suitcase full of things the day it happened. I was still in denial. In my mind, I was going to get home after all of this and everything was just going to be a great, big, giant misunderstanding. He would come home from work, like he always did, and life would go on, just like normal. I wanted to feel normal so badly. I longed for it.

And then the medical examiner called. Aortic aneurysm. Death was instant.

That little shred of hope I had been clinging to desperately was now gone. I just sat there, staring at the phone in my hand. I couldn't find any words.

He really wasn't coming back, was he.

6

THE FUNERAL AND THE AFTER-PARTY?

"I know you feel broken, so I won't tell you to have a wonderful day. Instead I whisper these words to you, 'just hold on.' As the darkest days of grief start to get less, the sun will rise again for you."
– Zoe Clark-Coates

No matter how much I tried to avoid, hide, or deny it, the day of the funeral came anyway. We all got dressed in our nice new clothes and headed over to the funeral home as a family. I gave my children the choice as to whether they wished to come to the service or not. My daughter came but stayed in the lobby, and my son decided not to attend and stayed with my aunt. Honestly, if someone had given me the choice, I wanted to do the same. That may sound terrible, but nothing can prepare you for this type of pain. Losing your spouse suddenly rocks you to your very foundation and normal protocol doesn't apply here.

No number of thoughtful cards, beautiful flower arrangements, or people visiting could make up for his absence. I didn't want to hear "I'm sorry for your loss" ever again. I didn't want to face a bunch of people, even if they were loved ones, family, and friends. I knew they meant well, but I didn't want to be strong anymore. I didn't want to break down anymore. I wanted to run away and pretend this wasn't my actual life. I had lost so much weight at this point from not eating and not taking care of myself. I had zero appetite and I hadn't slept in days. I was definitely not feeling like my best self. I didn't want to cry anymore. I felt like I had nothing left in me. I didn't know what to say. I didn't know what to do. I wanted to go home, crawl into bed, and never get out. My husband was gone. He was here Monday, and now he's gone.

We arrived at the funeral home and the family was able to go into the room before the service. I didn't want to see him again like that, lying there with no life. It wasn't how I wanted to remember him. I still didn't want to accept the fact that I was there for my husband's funeral. I kept circling the area, avoiding the room, and making small talk about nonsense things until the last possible moment.

I finally worked up the nerve to walk in right before the service began. I watched person after person approach his casket. Some cried, some smiled, and some shared memories. I shook numerous hands and hugged enough people to last me a lifetime. I saw people I hadn't seen in years; friends, family, and coworkers from the past and present. I cried more tears than I thought was even humanly possible. The foggy haze was still ever present and I still thought at any moment someone was going to shake me awake. It was both physically and emotionally exhausting, but I survived by the grace of God alone.

When we were about to leave the funeral home, I was presented with Kevin's wedding ring. That moment right there felt like an actual punch to the gut. That's when I realized he would never be coming home from work again. I would never hear his voice on the other end of the phone. I would never get to hold his hand again in the car or hear him laugh or yell "Jennifer" from the other room. I would never come home to him floating on the pool raft with the kids splashing around him. There would be no more seeing him watch the Eagles games in the back room. There would be no more birthdays or anniversaries. There was no more us. It was just me now. I was now alone in this big world, and I was terrified.

I somehow made it to the car, and then I lost complete control of my emotions. All of the pain that had built up over the past few days poured out of me for what seemed like forever. I sat in the parking lot with a van full of people and I wailed. My body was heaving and I couldn't stop it. My heart was broken and I had no idea how to even begin to fix it.

After I was able to regain some composure, we went back to my in-law's house for a gathering. I don't even know what you call what happens after a funeral. After-party?

Celebration of life? Repass? I'm sure there is a more politically correct term for it, but I can't come up with one right now, so gathering it is.

As I had feared, people kept saying things like, "This must be so hard for you," "He was so young," "This was so sudden," or my all-time favorite, "You're so young, you'll meet someone else." I didn't know how to respond. Uh, thanks? I know they didn't know what to say and they meant well, but there really isn't anything that fits here.

You should have seen the look on my face when my mom said I would need to write thank you cards for those who helped with food, sent floral arrangements, and the like. You don't even get a break from social etiquette during a time of mourning? Ugh, okay. I added that to my ever-growing "I don't want to do list" in my mind.

I'm not a huge fan of crowds. Previously, social situations proved to be a tad awkward for me, so given the circumstances, I was fairly certain that this one was not going to go smoothly. How is one supposed to act after her husband's funeral? Like I said before, all I wanted to do was crawl into bed, pull the covers up over my head, and repeat that process forever, for the rest of my days here on earth. I didn't want to be social. Nothing felt like it was "the right thing to do" in the moment. I remember sitting on the bed in the guest room at one point during the day and hoping no one would notice my absence, repeating the question to God again, "Why is this happening to me?"

I think now is an important part of the story to mention that throughout most of my life, I have battled with depression in one form or another. I was not formally diagnosed until after I had my daughter, when I was officially given the label of postpartum depression, but I can remember being a little girl and realizing that my feelings were a little different than most.

It started with intense feelings of being sad and alone, with no real reason behind it. I could never understand why I had such dark feelings. I had a loving family and lots of friends. I had a great childhood. I got good grades in school, played sports, and had boyfriends. I had a lot of things going for me, so I felt like I shouldn't feel so sad, like it was wrong. In spite of all that seemed to be going well in my life, I lost interest in anything and everything very quickly. I felt I couldn't control my emotions the way others could. I couldn't handle being criticized. When I got mad, it would take over my whole body. The same thing would happen when I felt sad.

I knew I was different, so I found ways to hide it. When I felt this way, I isolated myself socially and withdrew from those around me. I felt like no one cared either way. No one really knew the real me, just the me I chose to portray in public. Behind closed doors, I would have periods of excessive crying, followed by feelings of hopelessness, and then times of feeling nothing at all. I suffered from terrible mood swings, loss of concentration and focus, and even suicidal thoughts. Because I felt there was no real reason for me to feel the way I did, I felt ashamed and didn't feel comfortable asking anyone for help. I kept up this cycle for many years. The cycle went like this: feel sad and lonely, try to fake happiness, feel worthless, want to end it, climb my way out of it, repeat.

After my daughter was born, it got really bad. I realized I couldn't take care of both myself and her, so I finally sought help from a doctor. My diagnosis came back as clinical depression. I was told to take the prescribed antidepressant and try counseling. I tried that route for quite a while, but didn't have much luck. I eventually quit both, learned to live with it, and figured out how to hide it even better than before.

In the past, living with depression felt like waking up every single day in a hole. No matter the kind of day, it required significant effort for me to feel "slightly normal."

There were good days, days when things went well. I had some hope that maybe life was going to take a turn for the better. All I had to do on these days was take a little step to get out of the hole. I could dust off a little and go about the day. Not that bad at all.

Other days, usually depending on external circumstances unfortunately, I would wake up a little deeper in, and it required a little more work to get myself out. I started out feeling a little off, but it was still manageable. With some minor convincing, I could get up and play the part. There was some resistance and some withdrawal, but I was usually able to shake it off for the most part.

Then there were days where I felt like I was slipping down further and needed a lifeline. At this point, I would sometimes reach out to someone. Usually with a little help from a friend, I would be able to get out. They would throw me a rope to climb up and remind me I was needed and loved. I could still smile, laugh, and be able to still be a functioning member of society.

And then there were the really bad days...

Those were the days when I would feel so far in the hole that I couldn't see the light of day anymore. I would just get tired of trying to climb out. On those days, I would feel like all hope was gone.

During the awful days, there was a battle raging in my mind where I felt I was a worthless being who didn't deserve to breathe the air. Rationally, I knew it wasn't true, but I felt lost, alone, and like I had no purpose. I would be thoroughly convinced that no one cared for me and that I would never amount to anything. On those days, I wasn't even sad anymore. It was something beyond that. It would take every ounce of my being to just get out of bed. I couldn't even muster up a fake smile.

Understandably so, Kevin's death was the start of a series of the really bad, awful days. I could feel the cloud of depression creeping in. I didn't have the strength to fight it this time. The conditions were perfect for it to sink its claws in.

After everyone had left and I said my final goodbyes, I found myself alone in the back room. Sitting on the edge of the bed, I thought to myself, "That's it. I will never see him again. I'm a widow now." And in that moment, I had no idea what that meant for me or what I was supposed to do. I could feel the hole swallowing me up.

WIDOW

"If I called myself a widow, that meant that my husband was no longer my husband. He was my late husband. It was acceptance that he was never going to introduce me as his wife in a crowded room ever again."
— S.S. Jubilee

Before it happened to me personally, when I thought of a widow, I pictured someone much older and perennially dressed in black. A woman who lived in perpetual mourning, doomed to a life of sorrow. I felt they were never allowed to know or feel love again, show happiness, or celebrate life. I saw widowhood as the epitome of sadness.

I don't know why I had that picture in my mind, really. I guess it was what society had painted for me with movies and stories. I had other references. My mother and both grandmothers were younger widows, as they all lost their husbands in their fifties. I don't think I ever saw any of them wearing all-black clothing. I'm almost sure none of them had a black veil or a dress made of black lace stowed away in the closet. They still participated in everyday life. However, even as a little girl, I could see that it changed them. Their hearts hardened a little. A part of them broke and they never were quite the same after their losses. With their husbands, a piece of them died, too. My nana didn't smile as much, and she carried a coldness and anger with her that wasn't there before. My mom-mom left for a while and went to Florida because she couldn't be home after the loss of my pop-pop. She cried a lot and would forget things often. My mom stopped doing a lot of the things she used to do and seemed to worry a lot more. It was clear that life changed drastically for all of them in different ways.

It caught me so off guard the first time I was ever referred to as a widow. I called Kevin's place of employment from the hospital to let them know what had happened earlier that morning. I spoke to his manager and was given a survivor's benefit line to call. I was told I would have to identify myself as Kevin's widow and then they would walk me through the bereavement process. They were there to help me with benefits, life insurance, and any other necessary paperwork. (I was thankful to learn that Kevin had signed up for this unbeknownst to me). His manager offered his condolences and asked for information about the funeral arrangements so they could attend.

After we hung up, I just stood there looking at the phone in my hand. I had to identify myself as "Kevin's widow." Those words kept echoing in my head. They stung my heart. A tear fell down my cheek. I was Kevin's wife. I didn't want to be his widow.

I have tried to articulate what being a widow feels like. There isn't really a one-size-fits-all description. The best I have been able to come up with is the following:

Imagine your life exactly as it is today. Focus on that picture in your mind, nice and clear. Your husband, your children, your home, your friends, your family, your career. Picture it all. Think of all of the time and effort you have put into this picture, the years together, and all that you have built.

Now, light a match and set it on fire.

Watch your entire life go up in flames.

Try to extinguish it with your bare hands and a garden hose.

You may be able to salvage some of it.

Most of it is just gone.

There isn't one piece that the flames or water didn't touch.

Anything that may be left is damaged in some way.

There is ash and soot on everything.

Everything smells like smoke.

The water has soaked through what remains.

Now try to put everything back together when the other half of you is missing. Try to make sense of it all while everyone else is going on with their normal routines. You are forced into a new routine now. One that is foreign and completely unfamiliar. One you didn't ask to be a part of and didn't have a chance to prepare for.

While your friends are still having date nights, you get to do things such as find out where the Register of Wills is located. While your family is still planning Sunday dinners, you have to learn how to open an estate. While your kids still have chorus concerts, you get to figure out how to sell cars that aren't in your name. While everyone else around you still have their normal routines, you get to make phone calls to banks, credit card companies, and the like. You get to say the same words over and over again, "My husband passed away," which then is usually followed by "I'm sorry for your loss." "Thanks, I'm sorry for my loss too."

You get to stare at toothbrushes and shampoo in the bathroom that you know won't get used anymore. You get to fold clothes that were left in the dryer that will never be worn again. You get to look at the left side of the closet at all of the ties that you don't know what to do with. You get to move his coffee cup out of the way to get to your own because you can't fathom getting rid of it. You get to open mail that isn't yours. You get to lie in a bed that is now way too big and cold. You get to look at magazines that weren't meant for you and erase television shows off the DVR that will never get watched. You get to cancel dentist appointments and throw out cereal that isn't yours. You get to somehow learn how to cut grass and fix leaky faucets because it's your job now.

And this goes on and on for the rest of your life, because regardless of how much time passes, it doesn't go away.

It becomes who you are.

You can't run from it.

You can't hide from it.

There is no going back from here.

It's a club that you don't want a membership to, and only those that have been through it can fully understand its magnitude.

You are now a widow.

LIVING WITH GRIEF

*"Grief is such a lonely thing. There is no-one in it with you –
others may grieve for the same soul, but they do not grieve
exactly for what you also grieve. No-one has lost precisely
what you have lost. Not exactly, never exactly.
We are in it alone."*
– Susan Fletcher

It wasn't long after we left the funeral home that the loss
became very real and I realized that this was now my life. I
needed to learn how to live with this terrible monster called
grief that had taken Kevin's place in our home. We couldn't
avoid the inevitable forever. I decided that the kids and I
needed to find some sort of routine to help us try to put the
pieces back together. Grief was a part of our family now. My
role had changed from wife to widow, and I had to figure out
what that meant for us as a family. I started with research
to learn all I could about the subject.

Some researchers say there are five very distinct stages of grief:

1) Shock/Denial
2) Anger
3) Bargaining
4) Depression
5) Acceptance

Some will even lead you to believe that all of these stages happen in a nice, neat order, and once you reach the acceptance stage, boom, all is perfect in your world again. If you read the books, you may believe that you can wrap up grief like a neat little package, tie it with a bow, and put it on the shelf. I'm not disagreeing with the research. This may be how it goes for some, but this was not how my experience went. Not even close.

I have been in, or at least briefly visited, each one of the above-mentioned stages. There were also about five million other feelings and stages that went along with it. There was no straight, defined path. There has been no neat package at the end. It has been more like a tangled web of emotions that also included abandonment, numbness, resentment, inadequacy, betrayal, incredible loneliness, rage, anxiety, dread, depression, helplessness, low self-esteem, distrust, anguish, jealousy, and hate, just to name a few.

I liken grief to a plate of spaghetti. The grief is the sauce and the noodles are your life. It would have been nice if I could have kept things compartmentalized in nice neat boxes. Instead, everything got overlapped and intertwined, and the sauce got all over everything. It got on my kids, my family, my career, and my friendships. Everything was affected in some way. There was no escaping it. Some places were obviously worse, like my home, for instance. Home went from a safe place where we built memories as a family, to a place where I was triggered at every turn. It felt like I was walking through a minefield. I never knew what would set me off or when.

I stayed in shock for several weeks. As I mentioned before, shock or denial is what helps us survive the loss. However, when you are in this stage, that's it—literally just survival. I was not a productive member of society. I was not a good mom, friend, daughter, or anything really. I was floundering, to say the least. Nothing made sense or had meaning. Even the smallest task seemed completely overwhelming. I struggled with my purpose. I couldn't remember simple things, like where I put my keys. Appointments were getting missed. This was hard because I used to pride myself on having my stuff together. Now I was lucky if I remembered to eat.

Denial became a way to pace my feelings. If I pretended everything was fine, I could manage for a short while. If everything hit me at once, I would shut down. I felt like I was stuck repeating the cycle. I'm sure you have heard the saying, "Grief comes in waves." We aren't designed to handle that kind of pain all at once.

There were days it took every ounce of energy I had to move from the bed to the couch. It was near close to a miracle if I even brushed my teeth and showered. You know those dreams where you feel like you can't move or you're stuck in mud? It felt like that, but times a million. Each night, I would go to bed hoping the next day would be better. However, each morning, I would wake up, roll over, realize he wasn't there, and relive it all over again. It was a terrible way to live. If you can even call that living. I wanted the cycle of pain to end so badly, but I couldn't see any way out at that time.

I had to go back to work at the end of August. It had been a month and a half since Kevin's passing. Since the employee handbook says you get five days off for the death of a spouse, I felt like I should have been able to handle the task. Notice I said should. I was terrified at the thought of going back. I can't even put a number on the level of stress I was feeling. It was way beyond a ten. I was suffering from flashbacks and panic attacks, which are both Post-Traumatic Stress Disorder symptoms. The depression was unbearable. I couldn't calm down or relax, even if I wanted to. I couldn't make sense of my new life, but I was now going to be in charge of managing employees and making sure that eight hundred children were fed breakfast and lunch every day. Perfect. What could possibly go right in this scenario?

The first school function that I was scheduled to attend was an annual welcome-back breakfast at the high school for all the staff in the entire district. The district includes four elementary schools, two intermediate schools, a middle school, and a high school. With teachers, administrators, custodians, cafeteria staff, support, and district office staff, there were several hundred attendees.

The cafeteria managers were in charge of preparing and serving for the day. I arrived early and sat in the parking lot, focused a little too much on my breathing, or the lack thereof. My hands were visibly shaking and I was fighting back tears. This had become my new normal.

I didn't want to face all of those people.

All of them looking at me with sorrow.

I just wanted to go in, cut some fruit, smile at everyone, and say, "Welcome back!"

Why is everything tainted now? Will anything ever be normal again?

After several minutes and a lot of self-talk, I was able to pull myself together enough to go inside. My mind started again. "Have the lights always been this bright? The air feels too thick again. Maybe no one will notice me. Maybe, just maybe, no one will mention the giant elephant that follows me everywhere."

I walked into the office to drop off my things, but I was spotted. Several of my coworkers came over and hugged me. They told me how sorry they were, that they just couldn't believe it, and asked how I was doing. I told them the normal lie that had now become my standard response. "I was doing well. The kids were doing as good as can be expected. Everything was fine." You see, no one wants to hear that you're dying inside, that everything has gone to hell, and you don't know how you will ever be okay again. That makes people uncomfortable. They want to hear that you are fine, so they can also be fine and move on.

Denial at its finest.

However, it takes an incredible amount of energy to pretend you are okay when you are not. It's only sustainable for short periods of time. I was able to keep it together for a few hours, but then it became too much. There were too many people saying the same things over and over.

I cracked.

Tears started streaming down my face and I started shaking again. I tried to remain strong and composed, but the dam broke. I had such a strong visceral response, they had to remove me from the area.

Cue the freak show.

The next thing I knew, I was sitting in a back office that I didn't even know existed. Surrounding me was my supervisor, my previous manager, a counselor, and someone from Human Resources.

So much for normal.

They mentioned short-term disability, handed me cards, and I was sent home and told not to worry about anything. How was I not supposed to worry about anything? All I could do at that point of my life was worry about EVERYTHING.

The job I had worked so hard to get for the past three years felt like it may be in jeopardy because I couldn't perform my duties. I needed this job to provide for my family. I was now the breadwinner, the sole provider. I knew I couldn't allow myself to continue to lose it like this. I needed to compose myself for my kids. I was all they had.

The next day, I was put on a leave (
work. We came to an agreement that I w
return yet. One of the stipulations was
counseling again. When I had tried counseling beiuic, .
like I was wallowing and trying to find a reason for the sad
feelings. I was talking in circles with no real plan of action
and no relief. I felt I was getting nowhere. I was not very
happy about the thought of sitting on a couch and talking
about my problems for an hour again. I'm not knocking
counseling at all. I'm sure it's wonderful and helpful for most
people. I just didn't want to have to face the truth, actually
open up, and talk about the events with another human at
a scheduled time each week. I wanted to continue avoiding
the subject altogether and try to pretend everything was
just fine.

I also didn't want to go on antidepressants again. I
know they work wonders for some, but I didn't really want
to go that route again, because for me, personally, they take
away all of my feelings. I become just a numb shell of a
person. I look the same on the outside, but nothing
happening on the inside. I wouldn't feel sadness anymore,
but I also wouldn't feel joy, love, or anything, for that
matter. I felt very strongly at this point in my life that I
needed to be able to feel in order to heal.

What I really wanted and needed was to find
someone I could relate to, someone like me who had been
through a similar experience and made it through. I needed
an outside reference. I needed to know that I wasn't going
to feel this way forever. I wanted to know that there was

some kind of light at the end of this dark tunnel.

I looked for support groups in my area. After some research and asking for references, I was able to find a hospice counselor who would work with the kids, but nothing fit for me. The only groups I found were with much older women who did not have young children and were in completely different stages of their lives than I was. They could feel for me but couldn't offer much support. I found an online group based around the book "Widows Wear Stilettos" by Carole Brody Fleet. They were able to offer some encouragement online, but the closest chapter was four hours from my home. With my newly discovered panic and single-mom status, I wasn't capable of the travel, so the support was limited to virtual.

My family and friends were amazing and really tried to be there for me in the beginning. They called and checked on me, visited, brought us meals, sent cards, and posted sweet things on Facebook. We had sleepovers, and they visited for lunch. I still felt included and I had a great support system. I would never have to be alone. Maybe I could do this after all.

However, as time passed, they all went back to their normal day-to-day routines, and the visits became less frequent. They had their own lives. They couldn't spend all of their time babysitting me. They could take a break from the pain and sadness. I had to live with it, every moment of every day. Over time, my sadness became too much for some. Some people were too uncomfortable with grief, so they avoided the subject and/or me altogether. The absence of Kevin beside me was too painful of a reminder for some, so they stopped visiting as well. I couldn't fault them or get upset. I didn't even want to be around me most days. Their lives went back to some sort of normal. Their everyday didn't change. I didn't have that luxury, but I couldn't expect the world to stop spinning because I had suffered a loss.

There were so many nights I wanted to talk to someone, but I couldn't bring myself to reach out. I needed a safe space. I needed to feel like I wasn't being judged. I needed to be able to cry if I wanted to, or laugh if it felt right. I needed to let my guard down and feel safe. I needed to still feel connected to something. I needed to just feel normal for a little while, but I didn't know how to ask for that. It became so lonely.

The pain of being left behind was excruciating. I would put the kids to bed and then sit in the bottom of the shower and cry almost every night. I didn't sleep much, so I watched a lot of television, drank too much wine, and tried to numb the pain. My neck was perpetually sore from sleeping on the couch because I didn't like to be in my room alone. Daylight would come and I would pretend I had it together for the kids and the rest of the outside world. I would drink too much coffee, take too much Advil, and plaster on my fake smile. If I saw anyone, I would say, "I'm fine, we're fine, everything is fine." (Fine, meaning Fed up, Insecure, Neurotic, and Emotional.) Yup. F.I.N.E. Most of those days I would send the kids to school and then lay on the living room floor, curled in a ball, until it was almost time for them to come home. I don't know what exactly rock bottom is, but if I wasn't there, I was pretty darn close.

I also had severe fits of anger and rage. Anger directed towards him, the doctors, myself, God, and at anyone or anything in my path. My sane self knew that it wasn't anyone's fault and he didn't make a choice to leave us behind, but grief isn't always the most rational. In fact, I would say it's probably the exact opposite of rational.

One especially hot afternoon, I snapped. I was trying to cut the grass, but the push mower kept cutting off and the weed trimmer strings kept breaking. The yard was Kevin's job. Why am I even dealing with this?!? After spewing some expletives, I threw the weed trimmer over the fence in the backyard, stomped into the garage, and then proceeded to break every piece of beach equipment in my path. Chairs, umbrellas, shovels—you name it—smashed to bits. Utter chaos all around me that matched my life at that moment. I saw red. I screamed up at the heavens. How could you do this to us? How could you leave us here? Then I sank down into a pile and cried until I had no energy left. This was not one of my finest moments. I can only imagine what my neighbors must have thought of me if they saw any of this happening.

I wish I could say that was the only time something like that happened, but I would have to write an entire other book about my mood swings during that time. My poor Christmas reindeer didn't make it through the season, either. May he rest in peace, or pieces probably fits better in this circumstance.

To protect my heart, I shut myself down emotionally. If something didn't feel right, I pushed it away. This included all of my relationships, not just with men. My friendships suffered because I wouldn't let people get close to me. I distanced myself from family members, coworkers, and even my children. I know it was all part of the healing process. It was misplaced anger that I didn't know what to do with. When I think about how hateful I was toward myself and others, I am ashamed.

My emotions were so raw that even the most well-meaning friend offering their opinion felt like a personal attack, and then I would shut down. When they would complain about their husbands not doing something such as take out the trash, which I am sure I did a hundred times prior, I would feel myself bubble up with anger and think to myself, "At least you have a husband to take out the trash." Like it was their fault.

I even got angry when friends or family invited me out to do things. I thought, "They know I can't get a babysitter, why are they even asking? It's not like I have help around here. I can't just leave whenever I want." Then, I would get upset if they didn't invite me. "I'm still here. I still want to do things. Just because Kevin passed away doesn't mean I don't still have feelings." I snapped at my coworkers who complained about little things. "Come to me when you have a real problem," I would think.

I hated when people gave me their opinion. It wasn't like they had any idea what I was going through, so who were they to say anything at all? On the flipside, when they tried to help, I felt like they thought I couldn't handle it by myself. I felt like I should be further along in the process or shouldn't have the feelings I did. It really became a no-win situation. Like I said before, not much rational thinking was going on here.

I tried bargaining all the time. I begged God to take me instead. I just knew he had made a mistake. I thought if I did everything the right way, then something would change. It never worked, of course, but it wasn't from lack of trying on my part.

I felt like I was losing it. I never knew what would set me off or what state of mind I would be in. I could be happy one minute and then hear a song that would bring me to tears. If I saw a paramedic while I was driving, I would suddenly feel clammy and have to pull over to throw up. Someone could say something, and I would snap at them for no reason. Making plans became impossible because I didn't know what version of myself would show up that day. It was a terrible time in my life. I was convinced this is what insanity must feel like.

Grief isn't like a cold or a broken bone. It doesn't go away or get better after six to eight weeks of healing. I knew I had to learn to live with it some way, I just couldn't figure out how. All I knew was I couldn't continue living life this way.

9

SOMETHING HAS TO GIVE

*"The saddest kind of sad is when your tears can't even drop
and you feel nothing. It's like the world has just ended. You
don't cry, you don't hear, you don't see. You just stay there.
For a second, the heart dies."*
– Anonymous

I was still so lost and felt so alone. I didn't want to wake up
anymore to the same nightmare of his last breath replaying
in my mind. I didn't want the responsibility of caring for two
kids by myself. I didn't sign up for this. It was too hard and I
couldn't do it. I wasn't cut out for it. God got it wrong. It
should have been me instead. I felt like every choice I made
was wrong. I felt like no matter what I did, I upset everyone
around me. I felt so much pressure to do the elusive right
thing, whatever that was. I felt the kids deserved a better
life than this. I felt helpless and hopeless. I felt like I ruined
everything. It was too much pressure and I didn't want to be

in the hole anymore. It felt like I wasn't ever going to get out. I was tired of everything and everyone. I didn't want to feel like a crazy person anymore. My mind wouldn't shut off, and I wanted it all to end. It was so dark. Very lonely and very, very dark.

I called my mom and finally opened up and told her how I had been really feeling. I was not as fine as I was pretending to be. It was all coming to a head. I couldn't keep this up any longer. I was tired of fighting and tired of trying. I admitted to her I couldn't live with the pain anymore, and in the darkest hours of night, I contemplated ending it all. I couldn't see an end.

She cried with me and told me she understood where I was coming from. She knew it was hard and I was doing the best I could. My sister was fourteen when my dad passed, so my mom, probably better than anyone else in my life at that time, had a bit of understanding of what I was feeling and what I was going through. She assured me that even though it felt like I couldn't do it, she knew I could. She told me I was strong and would survive this, too. She told me that my life was my own and there was no right or wrong way to do it. I didn't have to answer to anyone but God. She said all we can do is our best with what we were given. I tried to let her words sink in.

After I hung up the phone, I decided to take the kids for a walk once they arrived home from school. We went to a small beach close to our house to get some air and try to redirect my thoughts. We had never been there before, even though we passed the sign on our way home every day that said, "Beach 6 miles." We always loved the beach as a family, so it seemed like a good place to escape for a bit. I thought maybe I would find some of the answers to the questions running through my head as I looked out into the water. If not answers, then maybe it would just silence the noise for a bit.

We pulled into the large parking lot. It wasn't super warm, so we brought light sweatshirts to wear. I heard the seagulls in the background as we climbed out of the van. The kids kept asking why we were there. I didn't really have an answer, as I wasn't even really sure. "I just wanted to escape from my head for a bit" didn't seem like a good answer to give to two children who were looking to me to keep it together. I settled for "I've always wanted to check this place out" instead. It seemed like a good alternative. They had no idea the depths of my despair. Or maybe they did. I'll probably never really know, honestly. I tried my best to hide the tears and sadness from them, but I'm sure they felt it.

I feel guilty that I didn't let my kids see me cry often. It probably would have helped them to see how much I missed their dad. Maybe my daughter would have been able to open up to me more if she knew it was okay to grieve. Maybe she wouldn't have cried herself to sleep so many nights. Maybe my son wouldn't have needed to go to a counselor to learn to express his feelings and not have a meltdown every time he separated from me. It probably would have helped them to know that I was having a hard time, too. I didn't want them to lose hope, the way I had. I thought if I kept it together on the outside, they would make it through this and be okay somehow. You know what they say about hindsight—it's always twenty-twenty. I now know that no amount of trying to protect them could take away the fact that they lost their dad. I couldn't fix it then, and I can't fix it now. It's just a fact. I did the best I could at the time.

The beach was a little over a mile of a small stretch of sand with a long fishing pier. We walked the length of the pier and then came down and explored the sandy area. The kids picked up sticks and threw them into the water. We searched for shells and wildlife. We slipped off our shoes and sat with our toes in the sand. We wrote our names with one of the sticks we found and then watched as the water washed them away. We did normal stuff, and it felt good.

I stood at the edge of the water and hung back a bit as they walked together along the shore. They looked so small and fragile. I was suddenly overcome with emotion. It was like something grabbed me by the shoulders and shook me awake. I had welcomed the feelings since I was numb for so long. Maybe it was the grace of God. Whatever it was, I knew then in that very moment I couldn't give up. I had to keep going for them. I had to get a grip, regain control of my emotions, and somehow start to recover. I had to show them how to live. I remember saying these words out loud, "They didn't ask for this, it's not fair if they lose you too." Looking at my two babies walking by the ocean in that very moment, I made the choice. I chose life. I promised Kevin that I wouldn't let him down and I would do anything and everything I could to give them the life they deserved. I would rise up to the challenge of being both parents for them. I would enjoy life from that moment on, whatever that looked like. I didn't have to die with him. I felt that he wouldn't have wanted that for any of us.

On that day, my perspective shifted and I cried happy tears. I felt a spark of hope that I thought was long gone. I hugged both my kids tight—and I've hugged them like that ever since.

10

THE BUCKET LIST

"Hope is the thing with feathers that perches in the soul
and sings the times without the words
and never stops at all."
– Emily Dickinson

Hope

Noun

a feeling of expectation and desire for something to
happen

Have you ever lost hope completely? I mean the feeling of not being able to look forward to anything at all. When life has brought you down so much that you have lost your ability to remember what happiness feels like. When you feel as though you have nothing but sadness and dark days ahead of you and it's never going to get better. When you wake up each day and you feel like you are drowning in sorrow and you can't see an end in sight. When it takes every last bit of energy you have to get out of bed and you aren't planning for a future.

We all have hopes and dreams, things we are looking forward to. These are the things that keep us going through the tough times, the things we are working toward. We hold onto the slight possibility that it's going to be better than what it is right now. The list is different for each individual, as we all have different goals and wants.

Before that day on the beach, I lost all hope. I couldn't even imagine my future self. I just wanted the pain to end. Most days, I wasn't even capable of committing to dinner plans because I didn't know if I would break out into tears, start yelling, or crumble into a pile of panic. I couldn't imagine ever smiling or having fun again. It just wasn't something I could fathom.

However, I made a commitment to myself, my kids, and Kevin on the beach that day. I would go on. I didn't want to just survive the days anymore. I wanted to learn how to be happy and enjoy life again. I had to find a way. I had to start searching for ways to allow hope back into my life.

A friend of mine suggested to me that I should make a list—a bucket list—of fifty things I would like to do before I die. At first, the idea kind of made me sad because I couldn't even think of one thing. Not even one. Fifty sounded like an impossible task. It opened my eyes to how much depression and grief had become a part of my life and how much time they had stolen from me already. I had been so far removed from my feelings and any sense of normalcy that I had no dreams or desires left. I was so deep in the hole, there was no light left. I had no plans for the future. I was breathing, taking up space, and just waiting to die. I sat on my bedroom floor, gripping the journal a friend bought for me, crying as I read and re-read the quote on the front by Walt Disney.

"All your dreams can come true if you have the courage to pursue them."

I realized courage had been a major part of what I had been lacking. I had been so afraid. Afraid to die, afraid to live, afraid of everything. I looked up courage in the dictionary and wrote it in the front page of the journal.

Cour-age

Noun

the ability to do something that frightens one or strength in the face of pain or grief

Man, if that didn't speak to me. So powerful. Strength in the face of pain or grief. In spite of. I dug in and I found strength I didn't know was there. I embraced courage and allowed myself to feel for the first time in quite a long time. I sat up for hours making my list. It felt like it took me forever, but I came up with this:

My Bucket List:

1) Travel to Italy
2) Learn to speak a new language

3) Pay off my mortgage

4) Learn how to change a tire

5) Fall in love again

6) Go scuba diving

7) Ride in a hot air balloon

8) Take a helicopter ride

9) Get a foot tattoo

10) Pay off my debts

11) Take the kids to Disney World

12) Visit the Grand Canyon

13) Try on wedding dresses

14) Write a book

15) Run a 5K

16) Take the kids to the beach for a week

17) Take a tropical vacation

18) Learn to sew

19) Have Lasik eye surgery

20) Learn to change the oil in my car

21) Start a young widows group

22) Cruise to Alaska

23) Take a martial arts class

24) Visit Ground Zero

25) Sing in front of a crowd

26) Go horseback riding on a beach

27) Go sailing

28) Take the kids to the circus

29) Take a ballroom dancing class

30) Go hiking in the mountains

31) Swim with dolphins

32) Buy a new car

33) Learn to play guitar

34) Go to Las Vegas

35) Live independently, support myself and the kids

36) Have family dinner again

37) Find a church and work on my faith

38) Retire before I am fifty

39) Buy a beach house

40) Get in shape

41) Trust someone completely again

42) Go to Cape May with my mom and sister

43) Go camping in the mountains

44) Remodel my home

45) Get involved with The John Ritter Foundation

46) Make final arrangements for Kevin's and Dad's ashes

47) Be open and honest with my feelings

48) Get a massage

49) Plan time for myself

50) Take a vacation to the West Coast

There it was, the beginnings of a new life, written out on paper. I had no idea how I was going to make these things happen. It didn't even really matter to me at the time. I just knew I wanted to make them happen. I felt something.

I felt excited. All of these things may not seem like much, some of them even silly, but to me they were very symbolic. They represented a future that I hadn't been able to envision until that point.

After it was done, I felt something I hadn't felt in a long time. A very small, faint glimmer of hope. Hope that maybe life wouldn't always feel this terrible. Maybe there could possibly be an end to this madness. Maybe, just maybe, I would be able to find a way out of this suffocating hole. I held possibility in my hands in the form of a list of things that I had feelings about. This list symbolized new beginnings and a new life. I had the desire. Now, I just needed the right tools to make them happen.

10

NOW WHAT?

"The best way to remember someone who's passed away is to carry the wishes, aspirations, dreams, and heart consciousness of that person. They live forever in your mind, spirit, and inspirational actions when you magnify the power of LOVE and make the world a better place."
— Brian Cimins

I would love to tell you that my healing journey from that day at the beach was picture-perfect. From that moment forward, everything was rainbows and unicorns. Everything after that moment went smoothly and we all lived happily ever after. The end. That would be lovely, wouldn't it? But let's face it, that's not real life.

The day-to-day challenges were still ever present. The kids still got sick. There were still bills to pay and problems at work. I didn't get a free pass from hardships just because I was grieving. In fact, most of the time it felt like I was held to a completely different level of standards and even more was expected of me for some reason. Real life is challenging and remained messy. Even when things seemed to be going rather well, there were speed bumps, hurdles, and sometimes other mountains to climb. Life didn't stop. Those mountains proved to be a bit more challenging when I was carrying things like grief, loss, depression, and anxiety on my back. I was trying to find a way out of the dark hole. The problem was I had no idea where to begin.

Here is what I knew I could count on: my sheer will and determination, my stubborn nature, and the love of my children. I was going to show our kids that just because we had something bad happen to us, it didn't mean that the rest of our lives had to be bad. That wasn't set in stone. While God was ultimately in control, we had influence as to the direction we could take. We didn't have to let this one thing define us. It helped because I truly believed the best way to honor Kevin's memory was for us to continue. I wanted us to not just live, but thrive and make the best of the rest of our lives.

This became my new focus. I felt it in my heart that Kevin wouldn't have wanted the kids or me sitting around miserable and grieving for him. I would be as happy as I could be and enjoy each moment the best I could. I would show our children that it was okay for us to keep on living.

However, just because I decided I was ready to reintegrate into society, that didn't mean society knew what to do with me. I didn't fit comfortably into my old life anymore. It's like that pair of pants in your closet from before you had kids that you swear you are going to fit back into someday. You may technically fit in them, but if you're being honest with yourself, it's never quite the same.

To top it all off, there is no road map for young, single-mom widows. There is no instruction manual you can purchase to guide you through the hard times. There are no reference books and no one you can call to fix things. I was literally winging it in every sense of the word. My core family unit was forever changed. My friends and immediate support system were also grieving and going through their own processes and journeys. It was literally like I had to learn how to be a person, a parent, and a productive member of society all over again, by myself, from scratch. Things did not go smoothly. There was a lot of trial and error and many growing pains.

One of the hardest parts of trying to move forward in my life was the hurt of not being able to make the pain go away for those around me. The constant awareness of that missing piece of our puzzle was always there. Wherever I went, I was hyperaware of the damage and destruction from the loss, surrounded by reminders of a past life that couldn't be. I watched my children cry for the father they had lost, but I couldn't do anything to ease their pain.

Hard times do not bring out the best in us. There was misdirected anger and blame. There were raw emotions and fear. I watched Kevin's family mourn his loss, but I couldn't do anything to ease their suffering, either. In fact, I felt being there just added fuel to the fire. Showing up to events, knowing that my presence brought them pain, was a hard cross to bear. I wrestled with the decision every holiday. Do I go or not? Knowing I was a constant reminder of what was missing became too much for me to handle. In my mind, I told myself that I was protecting them. If they don't have to see me, they won't be reminded of his absence, so they don't have to hurt. I was protecting me too. Trying to fit into the old routine just made me acutely aware that he was forever gone from my life.

In all of my previous circles, I was missing a very big part of the equation. Most of my friends were "our friends" or "couple friends." I still tried to hang out with them, but it became painfully awkward to fit in. You can only be comfortable as the third wheel for so long. It became hard to overlook the pained looks on the faces of friends and family when I would arrive to an event solo. Not to mention, when everyone else is still part of a couple, it just reminds you that you aren't. They tried to include me, but it just wasn't the same. I was the reminder of what they had lost.

I had a few friends who were divorced, and they would invite me to do things. The conversations would inevitably become awkward at some point. They would apologize for slipping up and saying something bad about their ex, or I had to fake excitement when they were talking about their newest crush. I was by no means ready to jump into the single life of dating. I had been married for years, so I didn't have the foggiest idea what that even looked like.

I was having a hard time accepting that my marriage was over. It wasn't a choice that was made. There wasn't a discussion. There wasn't abuse or cheating. We didn't come to an agreed-upon end date. I didn't sign any papers. When I said, "Until death do us part," I didn't bank on it being so soon. In my mind, I wasn't single.

I couldn't relate to my single friends, so they stopped inviting me out, or I stopped going. Maybe it was a mixture of the two. Who knows really, but in the end, it didn't work out.

Then, there was the possibility of meeting someone new. Things had changed so much in that department. The thought of using an app to meet people scared the crap out of me. I really didn't want to be set up with anyone. I didn't want to go on another first date. No, thank you. That sounds horrifying. I'll just be alone forever, thanks. Not to mention the discussion I would need to have with anyone new within the first few minutes of chatting with them. It was so hard to feel normal in a conversation when being a widow would inevitably come up. Then I would get the "I'm so sorry," or "That is so horrible" normally followed by an awkward silence. There were times when I wished no one knew me at all so I could have the opportunity to reinvent myself entirely.

I hated that I couldn't find my place. I didn't want people to feel sorry for me all the time. I tried, but I felt like I didn't fit in anywhere. It got rather difficult to sort through all the emotions and logistics. Unfortunately, any kind of behavioral patterns that you may have experienced before aren't made any better by adding grief to the party. If you suffered from depression, it's magnified. Oh, you thought you had anxiety and low-self-esteem before? Just wait, you haven't seen anything yet. Trust issues. Ha! Can I interest you in a selection of worst-case scenarios? You'll forever be alone and everyone is judging you. It's like all your emotions got together and said, "Here, hold my beer."

I now had desire, purpose, and newfound hope, but I still felt like I was floundering. I knew I was going to have to make some changes, but I just wasn't sure where to start. My old life and habits weren't working for me any longer. I needed to somehow figure out how to create my new "normal." The thought of this terrified me.

11

TACKLING THE MENTAL SIDE

"Courage doesn't always roar. Sometimes courage is the
quiet voice at the end of the day saying
'I will try again tomorrow'."
– Mary Radmacher

Fear

Noun

an unpleasant emotion caused by the belief that
someone or something is dangerous, likely to cause
pain, or a threat.

Fight or flight had become my normal resting state.
My brain constantly assessed every situation for the next
perceived threat, always waiting for the other shoe to drop.
Fear became my new home. Panic was always right around
the corner. Depression became my closest friend.

There were times I would wake in the middle of the night in a cold sweat, unable to breathe, reliving the loss over and over again. Each time, I reached over to the empty side of the bed, confirming what I already knew was true. Loud noises and sirens would still send me into a panic. I became obsessed with losing other people I love. I would check on my kids to make sure they were breathing at night. I didn't want to be apart from them, so they stopped having sleepovers with friends and I stopped going anywhere overnight. Fear, panic, sadness, repeat. Fear, panic, sadness, repeat. This was my daily routine.

One of the hardest things I did was try to make sense of my emotions. I needed to gain back some kind of control over my internal struggles. You see, grief can make you feel like you are going crazy. Years and years of depression can make you feel like there is no other way. PTSD makes you feel like you are stuck in the past. There were so many ups, downs, and sideways turns. I felt as if I was on a carnival ride that I couldn't get off of. I could feel happy and full of hope in one moment, then utter despair and loneliness the next. I was desperate to feel some sort of normal. I couldn't keep this up, or I would need to check myself in somewhere.

It was the perfect storm. Research states that the likelihood of grief turning into a depressive disorder is great. It can be difficult to predict whose grief will turn into depression, but the risk is greater when there is already a history. Grief mixed with my history of depression caused me to sink very deeply and quickly into the hole.

I was afraid to reach out for help due to the stigma of mental health conditions. In recent years, there has been light on the subject because of some high-profile celebrity suicides. However, in the past, there has been an underlying message that it's not okay to not be okay. For the most part, I struggled in silence and put on the face for the world that I was fine, while inside I felt like I was drowning.

As if the primary loss of my husband wasn't hard enough to get through, I didn't realize I would also be suffering from so many secondary losses. First, you obviously grieve the loss of the actual person and the loss of the relationship and connection. The person was there, but now, they are gone. You feel their absence from your life. You miss seeing them, talking to them, and of course having them as part of your everyday life. That was to be expected.

What I didn't realize was I would also be grieving for the loss of income, help with parenting, and loss of physical and emotional intimacy. I struggled with the loss of connection to other family members and friends. I no longer fit into my old life. I tried to figure out how to deal with the loss of shared responsibilities. Saying goodbye to all of my hopes, dreams, and expectations was difficult. I felt like another wave of grief would come knock me off my feet again every time I was able to get my footing. I would be left swirling around in the ocean once more, not knowing which way was up. Counseling and antidepressants both had not worked. I even tried self-medicating. Nothing worked. Nothing felt right. I still felt like something was missing, but I couldn't figure out what exactly that piece was. I needed something else.

Then I discovered life coaching, and all of that changed. I finally found the set of tools I had been searching for.

I was terrified to go to the seminar. What on earth was I thinking when I signed myself up for a weekend-long immersion seminar called "Ignite Your Inner Leader"? I was definitely not a leader at that point of my life. No one should follow me anywhere. I was barely a functioning human, at best. My self-esteem was at an all-time low. Up to that point in my life, I could have written a very long book on things not to do if you wish to be successful in life. Yet there I was, notebook in hand. I contemplated leaving the room and sending an email later with some lame excuse as to why I had to suddenly leave and inviting them to keep my deposit.

I was surrounded by coaches and people who wanted to be leaders in their industry. We learned how to not take things personally and uncovered behavioral patterns. We discussed emotional needs and I discovered "the why" behind so many things. I was introduced to the concept that "I choose the way I feel," which meant I could choose to feel differently in any moment. Wow! I now had the power to rewrite the rest of my life and I planned on using these tools I just learned to do so.

Up until that moment, I believed that life just happened to me and I had no control over anything. I reacted to what was thrown at me and used behaviors that I learned as a toddler. Maybe they worked for me at some point in my life, but they were not working for my thirty-something-year-old self anymore.

I learned how to uncover behavioral patterns that were no longer working for me. Once I became aware of these patterns, I was able to start taking steps to change them. The first step to any change is to become aware of the problem. The light bulb was turned on. I left that weekend with a new set of tools and a new outlook on life. I had the ability to make the rest of my life the best of my life, and I planned on doing just that.

I started by writing these affirmations. I still refer to them to this day:

I am loved by those around me and, most importantly, by myself.

I am confident and courageous.

I possess the strength and ability to accomplish all of my goals and dreams.

I am worth it.

It is okay for me to have everything that I want, and I more than deserve it.

I also rediscovered my faith during this time. Faith in myself and faith in God. It was a relief to know that I wasn't alone, and I could turn my pain over to a higher power. I was able to trust that His plan is the best plan for us, even if we can't always see the reason. He makes good out of every situation.

This was the beginning of what I needed to finally get myself out from under the hold that fear and depression had on me. I finally started to feel like I had better control over myself emotionally and I wasn't alone. However, I knew there were still quite a few physical symptoms that needed to be addressed.

12

GETTING PHYSICAL

*"You gain strength, courage, and confidence in every
experience in which you really stop to look fear in the face.
You are able to say to yourself, I lived through this horror. I
can take the next thing that comes along. You must do the
thing you think you cannot do."*
— Eleanor Roosevelt

As if dealing with depression and panic wasn't enough to
tackle, the everyday stress of juggling my new existence had
also started to take a toll on my physical health. Not having
your other half to rely on for help with the kids, bills, or
household chores was affecting me not just emotionally, but
physically as well. I still wasn't sleeping well, and my diet at
the time was rather poor. I noticed my hair was getting
thinner, I was gaining weight rapidly, and I was tired all the
time. I had a constant headache and developed some rather
severe pain in my neck. I flip-flopped between feeling so

depressed I didn't want to leave my room, to so anxious I felt I could literally jump out of my skin. I was suffering from panic attacks. I finally got so fed up with it all that I made an appointment with my doctor. She ran numerous tests to check my thyroid, iron levels, vitamin B levels, and hormones. Based on how I felt, I was sure I was going to have some sort of terrible, incurable disease. Turns out, I had extremely high levels of cortisol in my system.

Cortisol is the hormone your body releases when you are under stress. It stimulates the fight-or-flight system in our bodies. It's super helpful when you are being chased by a bear or you need to meet a deadline. That extra boost helps you to get things moving. Ideally, after you have that surge of adrenaline and hormones, you are able to rest and relax and then everything goes back to normal. That had not happened for me. My body was stuck in constant fight-or-flight mode. That is not typically sustainable for long periods of time, which is why I felt the way I did. It was already causing high blood pressure, high blood sugar, exhaustion, depression, inflammation, digestive problems, hair loss, and numerous other physical symptoms.

Stress was literally making me sick. The prognosis was it would only continue to get worse if I didn't make some drastic changes.

My doctor gave me a list of supplements to take, but in the end, she said the only way I was going to find any relief was if I learned how to manage my stress better. It's different than a food allergy, where you can just avoid dairy and then feel better. You can't avoid all stress. Even good things can cause stress. My whole life revolved around stress at that point. How in the world was I supposed to "manage" it? She suggested some changes to my diet, such as eating more natural foods, limiting caffeine and alcohol, making sure I was getting plenty of rest, and trying a yoga class.

Just so you know, the only experience I had with yoga up to that point was one of those at-home workout videos. In the video, there was a guy on the beach who spoke in a strangely soft voice. He wore weird pants, no shirt, and put his body in positions that I wasn't sure were humanly possible. You know what I'm talking about.

On the ride home from the doctor's office, I remember thinking to myself that I was never going to feel better.

It's been real.

How in the world was stretching going to help me to relax? I loved wine and coffee, and I didn't want to give those up. How was I supposed to get adequate rest if I couldn't sleep? I figured I would keep feeling worse and worse until I couldn't stand it anymore. Now I was feeling stressed about how not to be stressed! It was scary that stress could have all these physical effects on a person. I didn't want to live that way. I just wasn't really sure how to reduce my stress, or what I was going to do to fix it.

It was time for me to finally take some action. All I really knew was at some point, I heard about those endorphins that would be released to make you feel good when you exercised, so I figured that couldn't hurt. I researched some classes, but I still wasn't feeling very social and a little unsure about the yoga thing. I decided to join a local gym and work out by myself instead. Same thing, right? For a few months, I went to the gym regularly after work. I walked on the treadmill or elliptical and lifted weights twice a week, but I was still keeping to myself. I maybe had a little more energy, maybe a little weight change, but nothing to write home about. Stress relief was zero. It was so boring and I felt like a hamster on a wheel. I had yet to try a yoga class.

I was contemplating getting rid of my gym membership altogether, as it was an extra expense and I wasn't getting the elusive stress relief that I had been looking for. It was right around this time that my kids had gone to a weeklong camp that was held for children who had lost a loved one. One day at camp, there was an instructor from a local martial arts academy performing a karate demonstration. This is where the universe got involved.

My daughter was so impressed that she came home begging to try karate. She said the Sensei, Mr. Howard, told her to come visit his academy and try a class. Conveniently, it was right around the corner from where we lived. I remember thinking to myself at the time: a) I'm not going to be able to afford this (single mom, single income) and b) I'm not going to have the time for this (one parent, one car). She was so excited and she wouldn't stop talking about it, so I gave in and we went to check the place out. I figured it must have been something special for my daughter to want to do it.

I immediately liked the vibe I got from the place, and ended up signing both of my kids up for karate two nights a week. One of the nights, I was in the lobby during their class and another parent walked in. We started chit-chatting to pass the time. We exchanged pleasantries and asked the normal questions. It was during this conversation that I found out she owned a yoga studio in the area. I asked about the class schedule and discovered there was a class at the same time as the karate class. I figured this must be my sign, so I decided to give it a try. I coordinated transportation for the kids with their grandparents and planned to go to my first class.

I dug my dusty yoga mat out of the garage, threw on yoga pants and a comfy t-shirt, and headed to the studio. I sat in the car for a long time, fighting with myself to go inside. I already drove all the way here. What's it going to hurt to try it? Nothing is going to happen. The kids will be fine. You will be fine. Just go inside.

I finally went in and found a spot in the back corner, where I hoped no one would notice me. The teacher came in and we got started. The music was nice and the essential oils in the air were a nice touch, but I found the first part of it awful and a bit tortuous, to say the least. I noticed on the schedule that it was a hot yoga class, but I didn't realize it was going to feel like I was actually in hell.

Sweat was running into my eyes and dripping into my mouth. I mistakenly didn't take off my makeup before class, which made my face look like it was melting. My naturally curly hair frizzed out all over the place. I was confused the entire time. I kept slipping and sliding because I had the wrong type of yoga mat. Putting my backside up in the air in front of other people made me feel silly. I realized I had zero balance, and I was stiff and weak. No matter how much I tried, I couldn't get my poses to look like the person that was beside me. They were all picture-perfect with their luxurious hair and skin, and yoga pants that matched their mats. I looked and felt like a hot mess or some kind of deranged lunatic. Everything hurt. I felt like an out-of-shape baby rhinoceros in a room full of elegant swans. The teacher kept reminding me to breathe, which I thought was so strange. Am I forgetting to breathe? I couldn't get out of my head the entire time.

It felt like the longest hour ever. I kept thinking to myself, "This is supposed to relieve stress? Yeah, this is not for me. I feel more stressed than when I got here. I must be missing something." I couldn't wait to get out of there.

Then, we finally arrived at the end of the practice, the final pose, *Savasana*. It's where you lie down on your back and do nothing. Meditation. Relaxation. It was the most glorious thing I have ever experienced while being completely sober. I needed more of that! Where do I sign up?

I kept showing up and I kept practicing, but I felt like I wanted to learn more. One day, I saw the sign in the bathroom. "Want to deepen your practice of yoga?" There it was, a Yoga Teacher Certification being offered right there at the studio. I never had a desire to teach anything. In fact, I had been spending most of my spare time actively trying to not draw attention to myself. Still, I wanted to learn more.

I went completely out of my comfort zone and signed up for the certification right then and there. After spending a weekend with the owner and another person who wanted to be certified, I dove into the world of yoga. We learned about breath work, chakras, the moral principles behind yoga, and the benefits of each pose. I felt passionate about something again and I was excited to learn more. I still didn't have much desire to teach a group, but I wanted the knowledge. Shortly after that, there was a 200-hour yoga teacher training being offered, and I found myself signing up for that as well. Why not? I was in it to win it.

Over a two-year period, I put in blood (not actual blood), sweat (there was a lot of sweating, though, a lot of sweating), and tears (probably more tears than sweat). There were a series of immersion weekends where I would spend entire weekends away from home and my kids. There were assignments and visits to other studios. I had to log practice-teaching hours. Yes, I had to overcome my fear of getting up in front of people. There were writing assignments where I had to dig deep into my thoughts and feelings that I had been trying to avoid. It was both physically and mentally brutal, but it was exactly what I needed at that time in my life, for it was what broke me open.

It was during that training that I met an incredible group of women and I built a connection that I had never felt with anyone prior. After one of the many long days of physical activity when we were all drained physically and emotionally, we all sat around in a circle. I had already spent over fifty hours with most of them, practicing our teaching voices, how to properly cue a pose, and perfecting our downward dogs. I thought I knew them all relatively well by then, but I had no idea.

One by one, we all took turns sharing our stories and what was behind the smiles: alcoholism, abuse, loss of loved ones, never feeling good enough, depression, anxiety, feeling unloved, eating disorders, and self-limiting beliefs. By the end, we were all in tears, but we all felt lighter. I vocalized things out loud that I had never shared with anyone else because I was ashamed. They didn't judge me. Instead, they embraced me. They provided a safe space to share my feelings and feel connected, which was all that I had ever wanted. It was in that moment that I realized I had nothing to be ashamed of. I had just been looking in the wrong places for acceptance.

It was an incredible breakthrough for me. All of the pressure of trying to be this perfect person hiding behind a smile had finally lifted, and I could just be me. We shared an incredible bond that still exists to this day. We were able to be our authentic selves, some of us for the first time in our lives. We were able to share our deepest, darkest secrets, with no fear of being judged. Instead, we felt loved and safe. We were able to bring those heavy feelings out of the darkness and into the light.

It was then that I realized the healing power behind sharing my story. Once I met this group of ladies, it changed the way I looked at a lot of things. I realized I wasn't weird or abnormal. I accepted that we all have something we're carrying. Rather than trying to hide it or be ashamed of it, I embraced it. We are all the same.

That was the beginning of changing the way I looked at things. My old way of thinking was holding me back. We all have a past and we all have things we think need to remain hidden. We all have reasons we feel "less than" and things we think if others knew, they would think less of us. There is incredible power in embracing and sharing, and by doing so, it gives others the courage to embrace and share their stories as well. That is where the healing lies. When you can say, "Me too" or "I've been there," it builds connection. That's all we really want and need, right? To feel loved.

At this point, I was still going to the gym after work, but it remained a rather soul-less and boring experience. Thirty minutes felt like an eternity, and I was hardly breaking a sweat. I enjoyed practicing yoga, but that was still a rather solitary activity. I would go to the studio, do my thing, and then leave, most of the time just saying a quick hello to the people I recognized. I still felt like there were a few pieces to the puzzle that were missing.

There was a group fitness class at the academy where the kids took karate. I scoped it out since they started going there, but I was too scared to try it. I didn't really know anyone other than the few parents I spoke to here and there in the lobby.

One night, one of the other moms talked me into staying for the fitness class. She said it was like nothing else she had ever done. She was right! It was the best workout ever. I went, barely survived, and thought I might not make it to my car after. Holy crap! What was that? The music was bumping and there were about fifty people on the mat. It was like being at a really great party, but one that was good for you. Everyone was helpful and motivating, and my body did things I didn't think were possible. I was dripping in sweat and my face was the color of an apple. My daughter even asked me if I was okay when we were walking to the car. My arms, legs, and abs felt like Jell-O, and it was an incredible feeling.

It felt nice to be a part of something. I began to talk to other parents and make friends with people from the classes. It was wonderful because I felt like I could be myself. No one knew my story. The dojo (the academy) became a safe place for both the kids and me. A place where we belonged. A place we could go where people didn't immediately feel sorry for us. A place where we could be ourselves. It was something new that the ash hadn't touched. It was something fresh and whole that wasn't already damaged. I have to admit; it was nice to feel some kind of normal again.

I started to have actual conversations with other adults again that didn't revolve around loss or grief. We made plans to do things together, and I didn't feel like the third wheel. I didn't feel like a burden or that my existence made those around me sad. It was so nice to feel like I was breathing fresh air again. I felt like the kids and I belonged to something good. It was something we could do together, and we loved it. We were getting out of the house again. We were doing good things for our minds and our bodies. We were making new connections. We were investing in life again.

13

LOVE AFTER LOSS

"Transformation isn't a butterfly. It's the thing before you get to be a pretty bug flying away. It's huddling in the dark cocoon and then pushing your way out. It's the messy work of making sense of your fortunes and your misfortunes, desires and doubts, hang-ups and sorrows, actions and accidents, mistakes and successes, so you can go on and become the person you must next become."
– Cheryl Strayed

A relationship is defined as the way in which two or more people are connected. Marriage is the legal or formal recognized union of two people as partners in a personal relationship. I did not have many healthy relationships before Kevin. We spent eleven-plus years building our relationship into what it was. There were good times, but there were also hard times. We invested time building trust, sharing our dreams, and sifting through old baggage. We knew each other's quirks, and we worked around or through them. We had some really great times and also had our share of arguments. We had made it through the seven-year itch. We already had the discussions about how it drove me crazy when dishes were left in the sink, when there were socks on the bathroom floor, or when the laundry was all over the room. I knew he didn't like when I gave him the silent treatment, he didn't like too much garlic in his spaghetti sauce, and we couldn't make plans on a Sunday when the Eagles played.

We had a mutual respect and understanding that came from putting in lots of time and work into a marriage. We had made it through family issues and financial troubles. We had survived two newborns and were entering the school-age years as parents. He had been there for me through the loss of my dad, which almost tore me—and us—apart. Our relationship had survived layoffs, multiple moves, health problems, and more. We watched those around us get separated or divorced. We saw each other at our best and our worst, in sickness and in health, rich and poor, and even those twenty or so pounds you put on after high school. The next chapter in our lives was supposed to be spent together to watch our kids grow into teenagers, go to college, get married, and then enjoy our grandkids. We had made plans to grow old together.

Then, suddenly I was faced with a day when those plans were no more. I was forced to accept his loss. The "till death do us part" of our marriage vows came way earlier than either of us had planned. He went on to be with our Creator, and I was left here alone, separated by death. He won't be there for the kids' graduations. He won't see them get married or dance at their weddings. He won't be able to teach them about football or give them advice. He won't get to hold his grandchildren. Our family was robbed of his presence when we needed him the most. I try not to allow myself to get caught up in the "would haves, could haves, should haves." I usually don't question God's plan, but it's hard to not wonder why things happen the way they do.

I didn't plan on being single again, yet there I was facing the end of my marriage. I can remember so clearly in the beginning, people told me I was young and would find someone else. I know they came from a place of love, but I thought, "That's not really how it works." It's not as if my car broke down and I can just replace it with a new one. My husband is gone. My other half and the father to my children is gone. My marriage is gone. I thought I was settled. It wasn't really as easy as they made it sound. Even if I did, by some miracle, find someone else, that person would never replace those things. Life would still be very different.

Have you ever tried to put a puzzle together only to find a piece of it was missing at the end? You look in the box, on the floor, all around you, but it's just not there. You can't complete the picture. There is absolutely no way. You can't simply make another piece that goes there. Even if you find a similar piece from another puzzle that may slightly resemble the missing one, it won't fit quite the same. It may be the most beautiful picture, but that one piece will always be missing. My life had become just this, a puzzle with a missing piece.

I absolutely despised dating in my twenties. Since I had little to no desire to meet, date, or have a relationship with anyone then, I was certain it wouldn't be any better now. I was in no rush to do it again whilst carrying all my new-found baggage.

Just think of all the great conversation starters.

I was a young grieving widow with two young children who were dealing with the sudden loss of their father. We were all in counseling. I was financially and emotionally unstable. I had stretch marks and extra weight in the belly that you just don't get rid of after kids. I also had zero free time because I was the only parent of two young children, and I didn't want to confuse them by bringing people in and out of their lives. Let's not forget to throw in the fact that in my mind and my heart, I still felt married. Even the thought of talking to someone new felt like I was cheating. I really felt like quite the catch.

Putting all of those other things aside, the number one reason that I didn't want to get involved with someone again was I didn't want to risk love again. Love to me now equaled pain. I couldn't imagine losing someone I loved a second time. I didn't want to ever feel this way again. It hurt too much, and there was no way that my heart could survive a second time. At that point, I had pretty much determined I was going to live a sad and lonely existence for the rest of eternity. Cue the dramatic organ music.

In my reasoning, if I didn't allow anyone to get close to me, then they couldn't hurt me and vice versa. I was still so angry, bitter, and snappy. I didn't even want to be around myself. At the time, I felt like I was honestly doing everyone else a favor by staying away. I felt like all I did was cause pain wherever I went, like some sort of plague or natural disaster. Everything I touched turned to crap. It became a lose-lose for everyone involved. I didn't like who I had become, but I lacked the tools to do or be any better, so I kept digging my hole of loneliness deeper and deeper. I was cementing my destiny of being alone forever, one brick at a time. If I didn't make a change, I was going to have to learn to get used to my new solitary lifestyle.

However, I knew deep down in my heart that I didn't want to be alone for the rest of my life, but I was afraid of what putting myself out there might open up. I felt torn. I didn't want to never feel or share love again and I didn't want to shut myself off. I still felt I had so much more love to give. I wasn't looking, so God intervened and brought someone into my life for me.

One thing I didn't mention before was that when I first met Howard that day in the dojo, my world started to change again.

Now this is going to sound incredibly cheesy, like out of one of those silly romantic comedies, but this is how it happened. From the very moment I met him, I felt like I knew him before. There was a connection between us, something familiar. I walked into the room and he was singing and joking. I felt comfortable. It didn't feel weird or forced. He was nice, handsome, and made me laugh. He already knew our story from being at the camp with the kids that summer. He didn't overcompensate or over apologize for our loss like most others did at that time in my life. He was a little flirty, but not overly so.

I left with a small smile on my face and a little flutter in my stomach. It felt odd because I hadn't felt anything like that in a very long time. It was like something inside of me woke up, something I thought had died too.

I felt a little guilty for feeling that way, but I brushed it off and went on with my day. Later that evening, Howard sent me a message. In the message, he wrote that it was nice to meet me and he would like to talk to me and get to know me better if I were open to that. I thought, "Why not?" At that time in my life, I had a few men who had shown interest in me. I enjoyed talking to them when I was lonely, but as soon as I had made it clear that I didn't want any kind of relationship, they would typically lose interest relatively fast.

Most people didn't want to date someone who was emotionally unavailable, didn't want to ever go anywhere or do anything with them, and actively pushed them away at every turn. Can't say I really blame them. I just figured this would be the same. This wouldn't be love. It wouldn't last.

On the contrary, Howard kept showing up and I kept talking to him. I felt like myself again around him. Even when I tried to push him away, he kept showing up. He didn't let me retreat when I wanted to. When things got hard, he didn't let me run away. He didn't pressure me into being more or less. I didn't have to pretend to be fine. He wasn't trying to save me. I was comfortable talking to him. I could be open and I didn't feel judged. We both shared things and he was easy to talk to. With other people, it just felt like they tried too hard. With him, it never felt weird or forced. It happened organically and it felt good just to be able to talk to someone. In a time when I wasn't looking, when I had pushed everyone else away and shut myself off to love forever, we somehow became best friends because he wouldn't let me quit on him.

Our relationship didn't develop in a straight line. The stories you hear about girl meeting boy, falling in love, and living happily ever after, that was not what this was.

In any relationship, especially as you get older and more experienced, you bring baggage, jealousy, and insecurities. You bring the ghosts of relationships past. With the added grief, it magnified all of it. I had already made up in my mind I was never going to fall in love or get married again. That ship had sailed. Been there, done that. Having someone in my life who I couldn't resist was weird.

There was the internal struggle—part of me died that day Kevin died, and part of me is still here. Part of me still felt like Kevin's wife, yet I have these feelings for another man. I wrestled with my emotions. "Is this wrong? Am I ready to jump in and try this again? Can I handle trying to build a new relationship at this time in my life? Is it possible to love someone when your heart is still broken? Does this mean I love him less? Does this mean I am dishonoring Kevin's memory in some way? Is it too soon? What will others think or say? Do I want to risk being hurt again? Can I be vulnerable enough to love someone again? What will the kids think?"

There were friends who told me I should go for it. There were others who said I shouldn't. There were new pieces of the puzzle that I had never experienced and would have to learn to navigate, such as exes, stepchildren, friendships, businesses, and partnerships. Mixing families and trying to work out logistics did not always go smoothly.

Getting to know someone and being vulnerable enough to allow them to get to know me was scary. I was faced with the decision of following my heart or taking other people's advice and letting him go. Was I ready to take a chance? Choosing to show up and allowing myself to be vulnerable enough to love again was not an easy decision to make, and I didn't take it lightly.

I agonized, cried a lot, and talked to my counselor about it. I journaled, meditated, and prayed. And in the end, I decided to follow my heart. I was so afraid. It would have been so much easier to retreat to my cave I had made. It would have been safer there.

This was a process in which I had to accept that the picture of what my life had been and what my future would be with Kevin was now gone. I had to be okay with things not being okay. I realized if I waited until I was completely ready, that time may never come. It was never going to be perfect. Nothing was perfect before, so why was I thinking it was going to be perfect in the future? I had to mourn the loss of what was in order to be open to what could be. I had to accept that I had the ability to love infinitely. By accepting Howard into my heart, it didn't mean I loved either Kevin or

Howard any less. My heart was capable and big enough to love them both, one as my past and one as my future.

Choosing to love again after loss has been one of the hardest obstacles. It has been a work in progress, as is any relationship. I believe wholeheartedly that I was given this chance to love again for a reason. I believe we are here on this earth to build connections and to love each other. Life is too precious and too short to shut yourself off from love. I am not going to take one minute for granted this time around.

14

REFLECTIONS

"It's important that we share our experiences with other people. Your story will heal you and your story will heal somebody else. When you tell your story, you free yourself and give other people permission to acknowledge their own story."
- Iyanla Vanzant

Fast-forward several years later, I was lying in the chair at the dentist's office, waiting for the visit to be over. As always, I shook my feet nervously as the hygienist prepped her torture devices. She looked over at me and asked what the tattoo on my foot said. "One Step at a Time," I told her.

"Why did you choose that?" she asked.

I started to tell her the abbreviated version of my story. I told her how I had lost my husband suddenly and was left with two small children to raise on my own. I told her how I had to navigate the ups and downs of loss, grief, heartache, and depression. I explained to her that I got that tattoo as a reminder to myself that I didn't need to tackle everything all at once. I needed to keep moving forward, even if it meant just taking one small step.

She had tears in her eyes and told me that was a very powerful story. She then asked if I had ever thought of sharing it. I chuckled to myself and said, "Funny you should ask that, as I had been pondering that myself just this morning."

That was when the seed was planted, and I knew I needed to write this book. I hope my words can help someone else who feels like all hope is lost to see there is still so much more life to be lived on the other side of tragedy. I want them to see that happiness is still attainable. I like the idea of working toward that much better than drowning in the ocean of sorrow and pain.

I want to speak from the heart to anyone who may be going through something. There is no right way to do this, whether it be the loss of a spouse, parent, child, divorce, anything. I will say it again for anyone who didn't hear it the first time, and louder for the people in the back. THERE IS NO RIGHT WAY TO DO IT!

You can read every self-help book out there. You can listen to all the advice in the world. There is no recipe for a one-size-fits-all quick journey through to the other side of healing. Whatever you need to do to survive is the right thing for you. Don't worry about what it looks like to the outside world. Don't stress about others and their feelings. Do what you need to do for you. Period.

That's the right way.

With that being said, I am not a doctor. If at any time you feel like you want to harm yourself or you are being self-destructive, it is a good idea to seek professional help. Don't be scared to ask for help. Do it as often as you can. I should have reached out more. I should have let people in. I should have said, "I am not okay. Will you please help me?" I didn't know how to communicate what I was feeling at the time. I didn't know how to put my pain into words. I didn't want to be a burden, so it was just easier to say I was okay. Trust me on this. Being alone and secluding yourself does not make the pain go away. Most of the time, it amplifies it and you end up drowning in the sea of your own self-pity.

I know from experience there is no easy way through grief. It is not something that you "get over." It becomes a part of who you are. There is no way out of it, only through. It's like your own personal version of hell specially designed for you, a place where you are tormented and where you can't turn off the pain or noise, not even for a second. It follows you everywhere and like a smoke cloud, it gets into everything. No matter how good your intentions are, you mess up. No matter how strong you are, you break down. No matter how long it's been, it's always there. A part of you that is forever and always changed.

I remember shortly after the death of my father, someone said to me, "Time heals all things." I wanted so badly to believe it, that if a little time passed, maybe it wouldn't feel like my heart had been ripped up and put back in my chest, held together by glue stick and duct tape. I waited and waited. Time kept passing, but nothing changed. After losing two of the most important men in my life, the passage of time has not healed anything. The losses still hurt the same today as they did the day they happened. However, with the passage of time came acceptance, a tremendous amount of personal growth, and life lessons that I wouldn't have gained otherwise.

Instead of giving myself the grace I deserved, I beat myself up while I tried to navigate grief, work, getting healthy, and being a great mom. I felt like I should have been further along than I was. I should have been handling things better. I would get angry with myself for breaking down, as if I was giving in or being weak. There was no need to be perfect. I had suffered a trauma. I watched the man I love take his last breath. My life imploded, and I was left to mend the wreckage. I was so worried about how I appeared to others that I forgot to care about myself. I wish I hadn't wasted so much time on the things that didn't matter, but you know what they say about hindsight.

It has taken several years, and I am still actively working through these things. It took a lot to build confidence in myself. I no longer base my decisions on making other people happy. I learned how to set healthy boundaries. I realized I can be the only one to fix myself.

No one says, "I want to be a widow when I grow up, or I really hope I get divorced, get cancer, lose a child, or struggle with infertility." Yet, so many of us are given these trials to face. Grief can swallow you whole if you let it. It's one of the hardest emotions to process. It is love with no place to go.

From the worst thing in my life, some of the best things have happened.

I am finally at peace and have started to heal my heart.

I could have chosen to be a victim when faced with this trauma. It would have been so easy to choose victim. I could have blamed everything that happened to me on the death of my husband. I could have milked it. However, maybe this had to happen to me so that I would wake up. It has turned the light on for me.

While I will always miss him and the life we could have had, I'm grateful for the life I have now. I love better— myself and others. I don't stress about that small stuff anymore. On the outside looking in, my life is probably the most disorganized that is has ever been before, but I'm currently in a much better place. I chose to rise from the ashes and make the most of the rest of my life.

I have been able to use my story to help others who may not be able to see the light yet. I am stronger, in spite of it all. I was able to take something nightmarish and instead, grow and learn from it. I was able to cultivate strength that I didn't know existed in me. The most important thing is I didn't give up. In the darkest hours when I thought all hope was gone, I didn't give up. Me, the girl who started this journey, who held on through the grief and fought her way through the grips of depression. There was nothing special about me. I just decided not to give up. If I can do it, you can too.

Howard and I got married in Central Park in New York City last year. We have moved into a new home, surrounded by seven acres in the country. We live there with our two high-strung Labrador retrievers and my two amazing and resilient children.

Abby is a junior in high school. She is an excellent student, an active member in the FFA and Educators Rising. She works as a Service Advisor for a local car dealership as well as the family business. She earned her brown belt in karate, trains in women's self-defense, and helps look after her brother and little cousins in her spare time. She is currently researching colleges she wants to visit this summer. She has plans to become an Agricultural Teacher and just purchased a goat for herself.

Ryan is also an excellent student. He is a junior black belt in karate and helps teach the kid's classes at the academy. He has earned several trophies and medals on the competition team. He has trained Brazilian jiu-jitsu for several years and just recently moved into the adult classes. He plays trumpet in the school band and is also an active member in the FFA as well as the Young Marines. He is currently deciding what high school he would like to attend next year and has plans to be an engineer or work on airplanes.

While I'm sure they are building their own versions of this new puzzle and life after loss, we all have done our absolute best honoring Kevin's memory by continuing to choose life every day.

Right now, we are getting hardwood floors installed, so our house is in total disarray. As I write this, I open the front door and am greeted by displaced pieces of my sectional couch. I am sleeping on a mattress on the floor at night during the installation and living out of a suitcase. Dog hair covers everything I own and I am ok with it.

Our family owns a martial arts academy where I teach yoga and self-defense to women. I also work part time as a Title Clerk for an RV dealership. This picture is far different than the one I had imagined when I was younger, all those years ago. It hasn't been easy, but I love it. I am embracing the chaos and messiness of life. One Step at a Time.

A WORD ON AORTIC DISSECTION

The aorta is the main vessel that transports blood away from the heart and sends it to the rest of your body. An aortic aneurysm is when there is a widening or a ballooning pushing out of a weak spot in the aortic wall. This condition can lead to aortic dissection, which causes a tear in the aortic wall, causing blood to flow within the layers of the aorta. Rupture happens when the aortic wall tears open completely. Aortic aneurysms are the thirteenth-leading cause of death in the US, with 15,000 to 20,000 deaths each year.

Pain is the number one symptom. Seek emergency care immediately for sudden, severe pain in the chest, back, neck, or stomach. The pain is described as sharp and is usually followed by a feeling that something is seriously wrong. There are only three types of imaging that can properly diagnose an aortic aneurysm or aortic dissection. They include a CT scan, MRI, and transesophageal echocardiogram. A chest x-ray or EKG won't spot aortic problems and can lead to misdiagnosis.

Family history and certain genetic disorders that affect connective tissue puts you at an increased risk. There are also certain lifestyle and traumatic events that can increase the risk, including injury to the chest area, drug use, and poorly controlled high blood pressure.

Aortic dissection is a medical emergency, and the risk of death rises by one percent every hour that diagnosis and surgical repair are delayed.

Sources:

www.mayoclinic.com

www.webmd.com

www.johnritterfoundation.com

ACKNOWLEDGMENTS

I would like to take this opportunity to mention and thank a few people who have helped me along this journey. My mom, Fay, you have been a rock for me and an incredible source of strength and encouragement. My sister, Brittany, thank you for always being there to lend a hand and an ear. My best friend, Kelly, I could always count on you to be there for a sleep over or a pick me up when I needed it. The Conway family, Kevin Sr., Franny, Cathy, Chris, Danielle, and Evan, thank you for being there to lift me up when I needed it and for continuing to treat me like part of the family. Abby and Ryan, thank you for being my reason for living, a constant source of joy every day, and my reminders that a part of Kevin still lives here on earth. Lois, thank you for your guidance with the writing of this book and your encouragement when I wanted to throw in the towel. Heather, thank you for having the courage to write your memoir and for providing guidance through the process of writing mine. Jessica, thank you for introducing me to yoga. To my yoga training tribe, thank you for allowing me to be vulnerable and show my true self without judgement. Kiera, thank you for opening up the world of life coaching and for your friendship and guidance. Bob and Sharon, thank you for the camping trips and for allowing the kids and I to have a space in your lives and hearts when we so desperately needed it. To my ladies at North Elementary, thank you for being a light during the dark days. Scot and Dawn, thank you for the reminder that God has never abandoned me. Lisa, thank you for taking the time to edit this for me and helping me to make sense of the words in my head. Susie, Christine, and Stephanie, thank you for taking the time out of your busy schedules to read my rough drafts and for being an amazing group of strong women in my life. Amy, thank you for taking your time to write a heartfelt foreword and for being a part of my journey these last few years and for being on my yoga team.

To my friends and family at the dojo, thank you for coming into my life at just the right time and lifting me up when I needed it the most. As I write this, I am overcome with tears of joy and gratitude as I reflect on everyone who has touched my life in some way. To ALL of my friends and family that have been there over the years, I appreciate each and every one of you. Your presence in my life means more than you could possibly know in this lifetime. I am blessed beyond measure to have such amazing people in my life.

Thank you, Howard, for taking a chance on a young widow and her two small children. Thank you for allowing me the space to process and heal and for showing me that it was okay to love again. Finally, thank you for your strength and encouragement through the writing process. You saw the heartache, the anger, and the many tears. Without your push, it probably wouldn't have made it to paper.

And finally, thank you Kevin. Thank you for our time together and the memories. Thank you for our two beautiful children and for the love that you had for me. I know that you are in heaven smiling down on us.

ABOUT THE AUTHOR

 Jennifer C. Steele was widowed at the age of thirty-four when her first husband passed away suddenly from an aortic aneurysm. She was married for almost eleven years and had two small children. She was suddenly left behind with a mortgage, a mountain of debt, pennies in the bank, and severe depression.

She is now remarried and a mom to two teenagers and two crazy Labrador Retrievers. She teaches yoga and women's self-defense in hopes to inspire and empower other women to follow their dreams and continue living their lives after loss. This memoir has been an incredible healing journey and she hopes to inspire other young widows or those suffering from depression to keep moving forward and ask for the help they need. She has recently started a blog focusing on daily thoughts. She also hopes to continue her writing career by writing other inspirational stories and self-help books.

Connect with Jennifer online:

Facebook: www.facebook.com/lifeisbetterwithjensteele

Instagram: @lifeisbetterwithjensteele

Follow her blog:

www.lifeisbetterwithjensteele.wordpress.com

59493510R00083

Made in the USA
Middletown, DE
12 August 2019